DEDICATION AND ACKNOWLEDGEMENTS

For Ollie and Ellie

I would especially like to thank:

- all those who gave their time so generously to take part in the recordings.

- Nikki Kipfmiller, Catherine Whitaker, Megan Crowe, Eva Schmidt and the whole team at Collins for their enthusiastic support throughout this project.

- Murdo MacPhail and Frances Amrani for their diligent editorial support.

- Teresa Miller for being such an invaluable sounding board.

- Fiona Walker for her support in the writing process and her memorable interview.

- my 'students' in Bristol and around the world, especially the many from UPM, whose needs and desires to understand English however it is spoken have informed the writing of this book.

The author and Collins would like to thank the following organizations for allowing us to record conversations for use in this book:

Unit 3
WellWellWell

Unit 5
Virgin Holidays

Unit 6
TalkTalk **TalkTalk**

Unit 17
Zoological Society of London (ZSL)
(http://www.zsl.org/conservation/regions/habitats/marine/net-works/)

About the author

Ian Badger is a highly regarded author who has written a wide range of published materials to aid spoken and written communication in English. He runs a training consultancy, Business and Medical English Services (BMES), which specializes in helping organizations and individuals to improve their communication skills in English. This work, which involves helping speakers from all over the world to communicate clearly and effectively with each other, has made him acutely aware of the need to understand English however it is spoken.

Ian is originally from London but now lives in Bristol in the west of England. He has worked as a director of studies, teacher trainer, teacher of English and communications consultant and is a regular speaker at international conferences.

Ian is also the author of *English for Business: Listening* (Collins, 2011) and *English for Life: Listening B1+* (Collins, 2012).

Collins
English for Life

B2+ Upper Intermediate

Listening

Ian Badger

Collins

HarperCollins Publishers
77–85 Fulham Palace Road
Hammersmith
London W6 8JB

First edition 2014

10 9 8 7 6 5 4 3 2 1

Text © Ian Badger 2014

Audio recording © HarperCollins Publishers 2014

ISBN 978-0-00-754268-0

Collins® is a registered trademark of HarperCollins Publishers Limited

www.collinselt.com

A catalogue record for this book is available from the British Library

Typeset in India by Aptara

Printed in China by South China Printing Co. Ltd

Photo credits:
All images are from Shutterstock unless otherwise stated.

Cover: Blend Images; p8: connel, BeaB, connel, bikeriderlondon, homydesign, bikeriderlondon; p12: © Fiona Walker; p16: Sea Wave; p20: CandyBox Images, muratart, Liv friis-larsen, Sea Wave, Gregory Gerber, svry, D.Shashikant; p23: Lesya Dolyuk; p24: Subbotina Anna; p28: Rido; p32: auremar; p36: Monkey Business Images; p40: merzzie; p44: Zurijeta; p48: Mihai Simonia; p52: Andrey_Popov; p56: Jiri Flogel; p60: MarcelClemens; p64: yxm2008; p68: My Nguyen; p72: Simon Krzic; p76: Galyna Andrushko; p80: covenant; p81: © Collins Bartholomew Ltd 2013; p84: sainthorant daniel

CONTENTS

English for Life: Listening B2+ will help you to improve your understanding of English as spoken by a range of speakers for whom it is a first or second language.

You can use *Listening B2+* in the classroom as supplementary material for a general English course, or it is also suitable for self-study.

Listening B2+ aims to develop your awareness and sensitivity to different speakers of English. As you listen to the recordings, you will note which speakers are easier to follow and notice why this is the case: speed, clear accent, lack of complex vocabulary and idiom, straightforward use of grammar. As you develop your awareness of features which make speakers easy to understand, you will gain more awareness of your own English and take steps to ensure that you become a clearer speaker. You will also recognize how listeners interact with speakers, which will help you to become a better 'active listener'.

Specifically *Listening B2+* will help you to develop the following skills:
- listening for the gist/the main points made by speakers
- listening for the exact meaning of words and phrases
- awareness of clear usage and structures
- your range of English vocabulary
- an understanding of the impact of culture on the language which is used

Listening B2+ comprises a **book** and **CD**. The book consists of 20 units, divided into the following five sections:

Section 1 Lifestyle

Section 2 Practical advice and information

Section 3 Attitudes and behaviour

Section 4 Passions

Section 5 Memorable experiences

The **CD** contains 56 recordings of American, English, Indian, Irish, Scottish, Australian, Korean, Spanish, Austrian, Chinese, German and Polish speakers among others. The ability to understand varieties of English is a key to improved communication in English in your work and leisure. The recordings are unscripted and may contain natural errors. These 'errors' have not been removed from the recordings. The speakers' views are also unscripted and reflect their individual opinions and knowledge.

At the back of the book there is:
- the answer key
- the transcripts of the audio recording

Using *Listening B2+*

Each unit is organized into two or three parts with an audio track number to show you which recording to listen to. It is recommended that you follow the order of exercises when working through a unit.

You can either work through the recordings from Unit 1 to Unit 20 or choose the units that are most useful to you.

Each unit includes:

- Exercises which focus on extracts from the recording where you can check your understanding of specific features: pronunciation, vocabulary, structure and how the speakers and listeners interact.
- Gap-filling exercises intended to direct your attention to specific words and phrases which may cause comprehension problems.
- Vocabulary-matching exercises to widen your vocabulary.

Using the CD

Some of the recordings will be difficult to understand at first, but the task will be to follow the main ideas expressed and to familiarize yourself with unfamiliar ways of speaking English. The recordings are intended to be challenging. If you work on them as suggested, you will see a marked improvement in your ability to understand English as it is really spoken and will develop your active listening skills.

Other features

In addition to the exercises, each unit contains several features to provide useful information relating to what you hear in the recordings. These are:

Clear usage

These sections focus on specific issues which can cause problems for the listener, such as complex grammar forms used by native speakers or non-standard usage.

Useful vocabulary and phrases

These sections highlight key words and phrases that relate to the unit topic. The words and phrases usually originate from the recordings, but extra material may be included here to help you improve your vocabulary. Use **www.collinsdictionary.com/cobuild** for extra help.

Listening tip

These offer specific tips and advice to help you improve your listening skills. They will help you to develop your awareness of different features of spoken English.

Speech bubbles

Sections set in speech bubbles highlight and give the meanings of key words and phrases. These may include regional and more formal expressions and cultural references.

COBUILD check

In order to help you to extend your vocabulary, key words and phrases from the recordings are presented, with examples taken from the Collins Corpus.

Next steps

The final section in the each unit provides you with some suggestions for further study. In most cases it refers you to additional listening material on the Collins Listening website: **www.collinselt.com/englishforlife/extras**

Other titles

Also available in the *English for Life* series at B2+ level: *Reading*, *Speaking* and *Writing*.

Available in the *English for Life* series at A2 level and B1+ level: *Listening*, *Speaking*, *Reading* and *Writing*.

1 EVERYDAY TRAVEL

In this unit
1 Two British friends have a lively discussion about the pros and cons of cycling in the city.
2 Two Indian colleagues talk about commuting to work.

01

A Cycling

1 Do you think cycling in towns and cities should be encouraged? Listen to the recording. Are your views on cycling shared by the speakers?

2 Listen again and number the pictures in the order you hear them.

3 Read the questions below. Then play the recording and answer the questions.
1 What did Mike see in the morning that reminded him that cyclists do not obey the laws of the road?
2 According to Mike (first speaker), who act like they 'own the road', cyclists or drivers?
3 And who 'owns the road' in Matt's view?
4 What is a common misconception, according to Matt, that drivers have about 'road tax'?
5 Why was a man in Australia allowed to ride his bike without a helmet?
6 Is it a legal requirement in the UK for cyclists to wear high-visibility jackets?

Clear usage: emphasizing a point

Matt likes to use emphatic language to make a point.
He uses 'will' as in:
'Quite often you *will* get bus drivers who act aggressively to cyclists'
(He does not say simply 'You get bus drivers who act aggressively ...')

He avoids reported speech:
(She) said 'We pay for the road, you don't.'
(rather than 'She said that she paid for the road and I didn't.')

He uses the present continuous rather than the less dramatic simple present:
'We're all paying. It's not just car drivers who are paying.'
(rather than 'We all pay. It's not just the car drivers who pay.')

Matt says: 'I think legalizing helmets could be an interesting path to go down.'

He means to say that he thinks **making the wearing of helmets a legal requirement** could be an interesting path to go down.

'Road tax' (also known as 'car tax') is paid by anyone who owns a car in the UK. The tax is imposed by the government, but the money received does not actually go towards maintaining the roads!

4 Mike and Matt use a lot of idiomatic language. Read the following expressions and choose which of the two alternatives has a similar meaning.

1 It's the other way round.
  a It's not the way you described it. ☑
  b It is just as you said. ☐

2 It'll start to pull out on me.
  a It'll stop near me. ☐
  b It'll move out near me. ☐

3 The matter is cut and dried.
  a It is all very confusing. ☐
  b Everything is clear. ☐

4 We were given free rein.
  a We had complete freedom. ☐
  b We were restricted in what we could do. ☐

5 I got cut up by a car driver.
  a I was injured by a car driver. ☐
  b A car driver drove right in front of me. ☐

6 Cyclists should never jump red lights.
  a Cyclists should never start cycling before traffic lights turn to green. ☐
  b Cyclist should never jump off their bikes at red traffic lights. ☐

5 Listen to the recording again. Complete the gaps.
1 They feel they have to cross a red light to .... by a car.
2 I feel like in this city there's .... for the cycle paths.
3 [...] now cycle lanes .... but you don't have to use them.
4 Cyclists feel that they have complete .... of what to do.
5 I think actually that there needs to be .... behind the whole process.
6 But there are always going to be difficulties .... something like that.

B   Commuting

 Neeraj and Krishna, who are visiting London on business from India, discuss differences between travelling to work in India and in London. Listen to the recording. How do your experiences of commuting compare with those of the speakers? Neeraj is the first to speak.

2 Listen to the recording again and match the correct definition to each phrase which Neeraj and Krishna use.

1	the tube	**a**	travelling with unpredictable changes in direction
2	to commute	**b**	the London underground train system
3	without a sense of direction (more common: with no sense of direction)	**c**	driving within white lines marked on the road to stop cars from colliding
4	lane driving	**d**	driving as fast as possible and too close to each other, usually in a bad temper
5	minivan	**e**	travel to work from where you live and back again every day
6	pressure driving (non-standard English)	**f**	a taxi which picks up several people who are all travelling in roughly the same direction

Krishna says 'there is much more semblance here'. This is not common usage of the word 'semblance'. Standard use would be: *There is a **semblance** of order* (there is an outward appearance of order, but this is not in fact the case). Note these other phrases used by Indian speakers which, in some other English-speaking communities, may be considered 'old-fashioned' or even incorrect.

thrice = three times

to go awry = to go wrong

Could you kindly help me? = Please help me.

Let us discuss about this. (non-standard English) = Let's discuss this.

Where are you put up? (non-standard English) = Where are you staying?

COBUILD CHECK: everyday travel

- I didn't want to **commute** 60 miles a day.
- The streets were full of **commuters** leaving their offices.
- **Cycle lanes** improve safety for cyclists.
- Japan has a fast, efficient **public transport system**.
- The supermarket is **walkable** from the town centre.
- The village is within **commutable** distance from London.
- She **took the underground** to Earl's Court.
- They had been stuck in **heavy/rush-hour traffic**.
- Security is being tightened at airports and other **transport hubs**.

3 Listen to the recording again to check your understanding of the key points made. Tick the statements which represent the speakers' views.

1 It is a long walk to the London office. ☐

2 Neeraj says it is a one-hour commute to the office in India. ☐

3 Krishna believes that drivers do not stick to traffic lanes in India. ☐

4 Most people in India spend less than an hour getting to work. ☐

5 There is a lot of pressure on drivers in London. ☐

6 People use their own transport in India because public transport is so poor. ☐

4 Complete the table with the missing related noun or adjective.

1	chaos	*chaotic*
2	reliability	
3		connected
4	transport	
5		unreliable
6	order	
7		late
8	commuter	

Clear usage: expressing a point tentatively

Note the measured way that Krishna and Neeraj make some of their points about travelling in London. They do not claim to be experts.
'It's much more simple, *I guess*.'
'*Maybe* some of them drive on their own.'
'*I suppose* you could be right.'
'*Perhaps* it would be better if more people walked to work.'
'*It may be that* people prefer public transport here.'

5 Make these sentences more 'tentative' using phrases from the box once.

I guess	I suppose	it may be that	perhaps	I think	maybe

1 Public transport in London is just much better organized, ...

2 Commuting can be exhausting, but .... it's difficult to live near your work.

3 .... there should be a law about wearing helmets and high-vis jackets.

4 Helmets aren't always safer – .... they shouldn't be a legal requirement.

5 .... carrying a child on a bike is unsafe, but does that make it wrong?

6 You could be right, ... but I'm not sure.

Next steps

Listen to more of Mike and Matt's conversation at **www.collinselt.com/englishforlife/extras**.

2 LIVING WITH ANIMALS

In this unit

1 Two English friends discuss the challenges and rewards of owning a pony.

2 Hussain, from Saudi Arabia, describes his feelings about dogs.

03

A   Owning a pony

1 Before you listen to the recording look at the box below to check that you understand some specific vocabulary used by Fiona. The vocabulary will give you an idea of what the conversation will cover. Then listen to the recording and focus on how Fiona uses this vocabulary.

Useful vocabulary and phrases: horses and ponies

a New Forest pony = a breed of pony which is indigenous to the New Forest area of England (in the county of Hampshire in southern England)

moorland = uncultivated upland with low-growing vegetation

Exmoor = an area of moorland in the south west of England

to be spooked (slang) = to be frightened

a cheeky chappy = affectionate term which Fiona uses to describe Bertie's mischievous, naughty nature. 'Chappy' derives from 'chap', a slang UK term for 'man'.

a farrier/blacksmith = a person who puts 'shoes' on horses and ponies

to pine for = to be sad because you are missing someone (or something!) so much

to groom a horse = to clean the horse's coat by brushing it

---

2 Listen to the recording and answer the questions.

1 Fiona's pony …

   a lives in a forest.   **b** is native to the UK.   **c** comes from America.

2 Bertie has …

   a got a passport.   **b** been to the USA.   **c** stopped looking at Fiona.

3 When Fiona returned from America, …

   a Bertie had lost three stone in weight.   **b** Bertie turned his back on her.   **c** she called the vet immediately.

4 Fiona thinks that horses …

   a are scared of human beings.   **b** remember a lot of information.   **c** never show their feelings.

5   When the farrier comes, Bertie …

   a   tries to bite him.

   b   tries to run away.

   c   tries to cause trouble.

6   'Fiona's donkey acts strangely because he doesn't get enough …

   a   attention

   b   food

   c   rest

3   Listen to the recording again. Ian does not seem to know much about horses and ponies. Choose the pieces of information which are new to him.

1   Fiona's horse is actually a pony.   ☐

2   By law, all British horses have to have a passport.   ☐

3   Horses need to have their shoes changed regularly.   ☐

4   A farrier is another word for a blacksmith.   ☐

5   Horses' moods can be affected by the weather.   ☐

6   Small horses are generally more intelligent than larger ones.   ☐

Clear usage: using a range of past and perfect tenses

When Fiona talks about her visit to America and having to leave Bertie for a month, she uses a range of tenses to illustrate her story. Note the forms she uses.

Simple past
I went to America for a month
I left him for over four weeks and when I got back…

Would for habitual past
He didn't look at me
(He wouldn't look at me)

Present perfect
I've had him for twelve years
The longest I've been away is two weeks

Past continuous
The vet reckons he was pining for me

Past perfect
He had lost two stone in weight
We had built up that kind of relationship

COBUILD CHECK: moods and being moody

• You're not still **sulking** about that job interview, are you?

• Is he really in love with me or still **pining** for his ex-girlfriend?

• She was always **grumpy** and red-eyed in the mornings.

• `It wasn't meant as a compliment,' he snarled, **turning his back on** her.

• Even though I was a **sulky** teenager, Tony made a really big effort with me.

• When they finally arrived they were hungry and **miserable**.

• Anna had been **moody** and unapproachable for the past week or so.

4 Notice how Ian questions Fiona in different ways when Fiona gives him some new information and he needs an explanation. Listen to the recording again and tick the phrases which you hear. The phrases he uses indicate surprise – real or ironic. Would you expect the same level of irony to be used if you were having a similar conversation in your own language?

1 Is it? ☐

2 Have they? ☐

3 What's that? ☐

4 He's got a passport? ☐

5 But does he travel abroad? ☐

6 Is this normal? ☐

7 So Bertie's always in a bad mood? ☐

8 Sorry, what's a farrier? ☐

9 So, it's not to do with his mood? ☐

10 Did you say that the donkey is a 'psycho'? Surely not? ☐

5 Now listen to the recording again and focus on recognizing the actual words which Fiona uses.

1 Yes, I've .... got a New Forest pony.

2 Actually, his .... is Rushmore Bertie Wooster.

3 So you .... when you're going down five, six times a week.

4 He just wouldn't look at me for two days and ....

5 And they remember things as well, they remember .... they go on.

6 So when the farrier's .... he .... all the ropes to the other horses.

7 And then other days he's like a .... not eating his dinner.

8 While the .... in the field, they must just get bored.

Fiona frequently uses 'actually' to emphasize that what she says is correct and, in some cases, to indicate that Ian is incorrect!

B **Attitudes to pets in the UK and Saudi Arabia**

1 Listen to the recording and, as you listen, compare your attitudes towards dogs with Hussain's.

Clear usage: offering constructive advice

Hussain offers advice to people who may be visiting the UK and who may be surprised by the British attitude to dogs.

Note these phrases which he uses:
'This is something to expect when you come to England.'
'Don't be surprised when …'
'Feel free to express what you think about that.'
'So this is something also to bear in mind.'

Some other useful phrases
Be aware that some people …   *Make sure that you …*   *Don't be afraid to …*

2 Listen to the recording again. Check your understanding of Hussain's account by ticking the points that he makes from these statements.

1 Muslims are not encouraged to touch dogs, especially the mouths of dogs. ☐

2 Dogs are often regarded as part of the family in England. ☐

3 If you are visiting England, be careful not to say anything when you see a dog in someone's house. ☐

4 You do not often see people walking their dogs in Saudi Arabia. ☐

5 Dogs are not used for guarding or herding in Saudi Arabia. ☐

COBUILD CHECK: pets

- If people want to **keep** exotic **pets**, they should get some advice about looking after them.
- It is illegal in some countries to **keep** snakes as **pets**.
- Some **pet shops** do not sell animals to unaccompanied children.
- In common with many **pet owners**, Minerva often finds herself talking to her cat.
- I must confess that I have never been a **cat lover**.
- Snowball was the name of the teacher's **pet hamster**.
- She **walks the dog** for at least an hour every day.

3 Here are some idioms about cats and dogs which you will often hear in English-speaking countries. Match the idiom with its meaning:

1	dog tired	a	a nasty comment
2	dog-eared	b	exhausted
3	a cat nap	c	tell something that is supposed to be a secret
4	set the cat amongst the pigeons	d	a short sleep
5	let the cat out of the bag	e	cause trouble and disturbance
6	a catty remark	f	someone who does all kinds of unpleasant work
7	a dogsbody	g	worn, shabby as a result of over-use

Next steps

The speakers in this unit have firmly held views on living with animals. Do you feel strongly one way or another? There are many examples of pet owners talking about their pets on the Internet. Amongst the most famous is a video on YouTube where a girl talks about her love of cats! Search on YouTube for 'I love cats video'.

3 DIET

In this unit

1 Two friends have a light-hearted argument about vegetarianism.

2 A nutritionist discusses food groups and the importance of a balanced diet.

05

A   Vegetarianism

1 In this first extract from their conversation, Freddy and Lily discuss why Lily became a vegetarian. Note some arguments for and against becoming a vegetarian. Then listen to the recording and compare what you have written with what Lily and Freddy say.

> Lily and Freddy have an easy-going, relaxed relationship and indulge in good-natured 'banter' as can be seen in the following phrases. Listen to the intonation of the speaker and the response from the listener. They do not take each other too seriously!
>
> 'I think it's a fashion statement or something.'
> 'And you became a vegetarian at three?'
> 'What about hotdogs? Well, when you're three you don't really eat hotdogs'
> 'You must be kind of lackadaisical, over-relaxed.'

2 Listen again and tick the statements which best represent the speakers' opinions.

1 a Freddy understands why people become vegetarian but he wouldn't want to be one himself. ☐

   b Freddy can't understand why people become vegetarians. ☐

2 a Lily has been a vegetarian since she was three. ☐

   b Lily became a vegetarian after eating a hotdog. ☐

3 a Lily used to eat meat when she went to friends' houses. ☐

   b Lily hasn't eaten meat since she was three. ☐

4 a Freddy thinks eating meat makes you over-relaxed. ☐

   b According to Freddy, eating meat gives you energy. ☐

5 a Lily makes a special effort to cook meat when entertaining her meat-eating friends. ☐

   b Lily only offers her friends vegetarian dishes. ☐

6 a Lily now eats fish, but mainly because she wants to be polite. ☐

   b Lily now enjoys eating fish. ☐

COBUILD CHECK: vegetarianism

- I turned to **vegetarianism** about nine years ago for moral reasons.
- 15 years ago he converted to **veganism**, shunning meat, cheese, eggs and other animal products.
- If you are a **vegan**, you may be low in calcium or vitamin D.
- At least more and more places are offering a **veggie/vegetarian** choice on the menu.
- Alma's not a vegetarian but she often chooses the **veggie burger** over the beef version.
- If you have any special **dietary requirements**, please let us know when you are booking.
- Many people have to follow **special diets** for medical reasons.
- I love chocolate and I would never **give up eating** it.

According to a 2013 survey conducted by the British Nutrition Foundation, one in three primary schoolchildren in the UK thought that cheese was a vegetable, that fish fingers came from chicken and that pasta was an animal product!

 Match the adjectives with their opposites.

1	trendy		**a**	childish
2	energetic		**b**	impolite
3	courteous		**c**	incomprehensible
4	tasty		**d**	unfashionable
5	adult		**e**	bland
6	understandable		**f**	lazy

B   Living as a vegetarian

06

In this second extract from their conversation, Freddy and Lily discuss the reasons why someone might become a vegetarian and some practicalities of buying and eating vegetarian food. Why would you expect someone to become a vegetarian? Is it easy to live a vegetarian life where you live? Listen to the recording and compare your thoughts with those of Freddy and Lily.

Useful vocabulary and phrases: food and lifestyles

Quorn™ mince = a popular vegetarian alternative to minced meat (see www.quorn.com)

to live a lie = to live a life that is totally dishonest

to fit in with the crowd = to be popular

omnivores = people who eat everything

processed meat = meat that has been transformed into a product, e.g. for the supermarket

[…] and stuff = and things like that (*slang*)

2 Listen again to check your detailed understanding of what is said. Are these statements true or false?

		True	False
1	Lily thinks Quorn tastes good.	....	....
2	Freddy does not believe that we eat too much meat.	....	....
3	Lily thinks preparing a vegetarian dish is more difficult than preparing a fish dish.	....	....
4	Freddy believes that a vegetarian diet is cheaper.	....	....
5	Freddy is a highly proficient cook.	....	....

Clear usage: adjectives and adverbs

Freddy talks about *'cheap'* food (cheap = an adjective)
*We can eat **cheaply** if we eat plenty of vegetables* (cheaply = an adverb)
This is standard use and most speakers in this book use these standard forms of adjectives and adverbs. Note however that increasing numbers of speakers do not use standard adverbial forms. You will sometimes hear, for example: *We can eat cheap if... .'*

He played well (standard) – *He played good* (non-standard)
He spoke English badly (standard) – *He spoke English bad* (non-standard)
He walked slowly (standard) – *He walked slow* (non-standard)

3 Note the interaction between the two speakers and how they interject whilst the other is speaking. Listen again. Write down what the other speaker interjects whilst the main speaker is talking.

1 I know that sounds disgusting …	..........*Oh yeah, mmm.*..........
2 It's got the texture of …	....
3 […] but I can see why …	....
4 Vegetarian food beyond just boiling	....
5 I think a balanced diet	....
6 […] increased my food bills by quite a lot …	....
7 […] kind of processed meats and stuff, or I find …	....

COBUILD CHECK: taste and texture

• The cheese **had** an odd, wet, crumbly **texture**.
• The sweet looked like a strawberry but **tasted like** a pineapple.
• I had a generous portion of pizza which was very **tasty**.
• I found the chickpea dip too grainy and **bland**.
• Rolled oats give these muffins a dense, **chewy** texture that makes them rather filling.

C   Good nutrition

Listen to the recording. What, if any, of the information given by Jackie is new to you? Is this information relevant to the kind of diet you have in your country?

2 Listen to the first part of the recording again and list the foods under the food groups which Jackie mentions.

1 Protein .... Vegetable Protein ....

2 Carbohydrates .... Complex Carbohydrates ....

3 Fats (Saturated) .... Essential Fats ....

Listening tip: explaining unfamiliar terms

Jackie knows that her listeners may not have the same level of knowledge as her. Note how she makes her message clear when she uses unfamiliar/technical terms by immediately translating specialized language into everyday language which she thinks her listener will understand:

'What we call essential fats, which are the Omega 3 ... .'
'We have something called 'micro-nutrients'.'
'When I talk about the wrong kind of carbohydrate, what I basically mean is sugar.'

---

3 Jackie signals some of her important messages by introducing them with words and phrases such as 'Now', 'So', 'The best thing', etc. Listen again, pause the recording as necessary, and complete the advice she gives.

1 So it's very important .... balance of all three.

2 The best thing first of all .... that you're having a good balance.

3 The best way to go .... it's complex carbohydrate.

4 Now, if you blend ...., then that's going to lead to ... .

5 First of all, sugar .... when it comes to weight gain.

6 So, if your lunch .... a white bread sandwich and a bar of chocolate.

Clear usage: 'if' clauses relating to possible future change

Study the sentences which Jackie uses below and the different forms of *'will'* and *'going to'* which she uses after 'if' clauses. She wants to give clear examples of how things will definitely change in the future if you make the correct decisions on diet now.

'If you *don't* get enough of one of them, there *will* be a knock-on effect.'
'If you *blend* complex carbohydrates with protein, then that's *going to lead* to sustained energy.'
'If you have a brown bread sandwich ... , then you're *going to be* getting fibre ... .'
'If you can think about having protein with every meal ... *you won't* be relying on coffee all the time.'

Next steps

Listen to the recordings whilst reading the transcripts and check any unknown words and expressions. Has the final recording made you think more about what you eat? Jackie goes on to talk about the global problem of 'obesity'. Go to **www.collinselt.com/englishforlife/extras** where you will find the recording and a transcript.

4 EATING HABITS

In this unit

1 A Turkish restaurant owner talks about Turkish food and eating etiquette.

2 A Frenchman who has been working in the UK comments on English food and eating habits.

A Mealtimes in Turkey

08

1 Listen to the recording. Is there anything that Serhat says which comes as a surprise to you? Compare what he says about eating etiquette in Turkish families with eating etiquette in your family or country. Do you believe that it is important for families to eat together as he describes?

2 Listen to the recording again and number the photos in the order you hear them mentioned.

Clear usage: expressing strong opinions

Serhat has a strongly-held opinion that families should eat together. Note some of the expressions which he uses to emphasize this fact. Where Serhat uses non-standard English, standard English equivalents are given in brackets.

'All (of the) family should be together.'
'Especially kids doesn't start (don't start or shouldn't start) (a) meal without their mums and dads.'
'If they finish early, no-one leaves the table.' (no-one should leave the table)
'They gonna sit and they gonna eat.' (They should sit and they should eat)

Serhat says 'there is sea basses and anchovies'.
Standard English: *there are sea bass and anchovies*.

'When they're in table the Turkish people love the speaking'
Standard English: *When they are sitting at the table, Turkish people love to talk*.

3 Answer the true/false questions from your memory of listening to the recording for the first time. Then listen again to check your answers.

	True	False
1 In traditional family meals in Turkey, mothers and fathers start eating first.	....	....
2 When you finish eating, you can leave the table.	....	....
3 Turkish people love to talk whilst they are eating.	....	....
4 Serhat lives near the Black Sea.	....	....
5 People in the Black Sea area of Turkey eat a lot of fish, except in the winter time.	....	....
6 Rice is not very popular in Turkey.	....	....
7 Lentil soup is frequently eaten as a starter in Turkey.	....	....
8 Children do not have to eat soup before they can start their main course.	....	....

Useful vocabulary and phrases: table manners

Please start.
Bon appetit!
Please help yourselves to salad.
Sorry, I'm not used to eating with a knife and fork or chopsticks.
Let me serve you some more rice.
Have you had baklava before?
Do try it.
That was a delicious meal.

---

4 These are Turkish words commonly used in English. Match the word with its definition.

1 Döner kebap		**a**	a sweet dessert
2 Baklava		**b**	a cap which covers the head and neck
3 a balaclava		**c**	a long-sleeved tunic with a belt or a long flowing garment
4 a kaftan		**d**	a tent-like dwelling
5 a yurt		**e**	meat cooked on a vertical spit which is sliced and served in sandwiches or on flatbread

B ## Comparing French and British eating habits

Listen to the recording. If you have lived in the UK, do you share Philippe's opinion of English food? Are you surprised by anything he says? Note that in common with many French speakers of English, he does not always pronounce the 'h' at the beginning of words or the 's' at the end of words.

Listen again and give detailed answers to show you understand what he says.

1   What surprises Philippe about the behaviour of his work colleagues at lunch time?
2   In France, what would Philippe need to do if he wanted to leave the lunch table early?
3   What is his attitude towards people who use their mobile phones or browse the Internet during lunch?
4   What English food does he claim to like?
5   Why does he think that 'traditional' English fish and chips is not a 'dish'?
6   Do you tend to agree or disagree with Philippe's attitudes to mealtimes and, if you have been to the UK, his opinion of British food?

Clear usage: hedging

Hedging is when the speaker avoids committing to a particular view or opinion. Philippe does not want to be too critical in his comments. He wishes to be polite and to qualify his remarks. He says:
'I don't (wouldn't) say I don't like it, but to me it is not a dish.'

Some other phrases which speakers might use when they want to be cautious about giving an opinion:
I can't really say whether I agree or disagree
I suppose you could say that, but some would disagree
I guess it depends on what you mean by 'English food'!

Listen to the recording again and check your recognition of specific words and phrases by completing the gaps.

1   People don't wait (for) .... to go for lunch.
2   That's quite .... This is the sort of thing we won't do in France.
3   So that's .... and quite impolite.
4   I don't say that I don't like it, but .... It's just fish with chips.
5   It is cooked with ...., from ...

COBUILD CHECK: meals and dishes

• Sophie had asked if she could help to **prepare** the **meal**.
• The restaurant offers **traditional** English and Welsh **dishes**.
• They rarely ate in restaurants because he preferred **home cooking**.
• We were waiting for Mum to **dish up** the dinner.
• They have **set meal times** — 9 a.m., noon, and 8 p.m.

4 Philippe does not always use 'standard' English. Note these examples from the recording and put them into 'standard' English. Do his 'mistakes' cause you any difficulties in understanding him?

Philippe	'Standard' English
[...] people don't wait each other ...	....
[...] before you have even finish your meal ...	....
If I would have to leave the table ...	....
There's no point to ask permission	....
Now not because I'm used	....
Smartphone is very often used during the meals	....

In the UK, the word 'pudding' is used by many, but not all speakers, to describe a dessert. 'Pudding' is also used to describe a particular type of dessert, such as 'Christmas pudding' (see photo below), 'bread and butter pudding' and 'sticky toffee pudding'.

Next steps

Listen to the recordings again whilst reading the transcript. Underline any words and phrases which you find difficult to understand initially. Then play the recording again. Do you find it easier to follow the speakers now?

If you would like to hear more from Serhat, go to: **www.collinselt.com/englishforlife/extras.**

5 MAKING ARRANGEMENTS AND CHANGES

In this unit

There are three recordings in this unit, all concerned with a booking made with Virgin Holidays.

1 Grace, from Cork in Ireland, books a holiday over the telephone.
2 She calls back to make some changes to her reservation.

A   **Booking a holiday**

1   Grace, calls Chloe, a Virgin representative from London, to make arrangements for a holiday in Mexico. Listen to the recording before doing the exercises below. How would you rate Chloe in terms of her friendliness and willingness to help Grace?

2   Listen again. Pause the recording as necessary to focus on specific information as you answer these true/false questions.

		True	False
1	Both Grace and Chloe have visited Mexico before.	………	………
2	Chloe enjoyed her stay in Mexico one hour away from Cancun.	………	………
3	Grace and her friend would like to stay in a hotel where they can meet people of a similar age.	………	………
4	The hotel where Chloe stayed had a bar in the pool.	………	………
5	Virgin Atlantic flies to Mexico three times per week.	………	………
6	Grace does not remember her postcode.	………	………

Clear usage: establishing empathy

Chloe is very professional in the way she helps Grace and establishes empathy. Note how she personalizes her advice by sharing her and other clients' experiences with Grace and thus encourages her to book the holiday.

'I've actually just returned from Mexico. It was a wonderful, so good destination.'
(standard English = *It was a wonderful destination.* or *It was such a good destination.*)
'That's definitely a possibility.'
'What a lot of people did …'
'It's totally up to you.'
'I would say that would be the best way to do it.'
'It was lovely.'
'I'm sure we'll be able to (kinda) fit that in.'

Chloe and Grace use a lot of 'fillers' in their language, features of everyday speech which in this instance create friendly and informal rapport. Listen to the recording again and tick the phrases each time you hear them used as a filler.

1 like   ☐☐☐☐☐☐☐☐☐☐

2 kind of (kinda)   ☐☐☐☐☐☐☐☐☐☐

3 say   ☐☐☐☐☐☐☐☐☐☐

4 just   ☐☐☐☐☐☐☐☐☐☐

5 I guess   ☐☐☐☐☐☐☐☐☐☐

6 I suppose   ☐☐☐☐☐☐☐☐☐☐

7 I mean   ☐☐☐☐☐☐☐☐☐☐

8 you know   ☐☐☐☐☐☐☐☐☐☐

9 a bit   ☐☐☐☐☐☐☐☐☐☐

10 okay   ☐☐☐☐☐☐☐☐☐☐

COBUILD CHECK: peaceful or hectic

- How do you **relax** after training?
- I am loving my stay in Scotland. It is very **relaxing** and the break is just what I needed.
- If it's a **restful** holiday you want, then this action break is not what you are looking for.
- Kate and Alistair had had a **hectic** Christmas with family from both sides crammed into their small townhouse.
- She loves the **peace and quiet** of the island and the idea of doing her own thing.

Listening tip: missing words

Note that native speakers sometimes miss out words which you might expect to hear. This should not distract you from understanding the meaning of what is said. For example, Chloe says:

'Have you looked at any holidays or got anywhere in mind that you wanted to stay or (are you) just open to kind of recommendations?'

'What we did and what a lot of other guests that we kind of made friends (with) did, they booked …'

B Confirming details

 In this second extract of the conversation between Grace and Chloe, Chloe confirms details of the booking made. Listen to the recording before doing any of the exercises. What information does Chloe need? What is the travel destination which was not mentioned in the conversation?

Useful vocabulary and phrases: language of confirmation

Wonderful	That's all paid for.
So, we've got …	Let me give you that booking reference.
Was that all correct – Yes, good perfect.	I'll just recap everything with you.
Right, that's just going through now.	We've got you staying for three nights …
Lovely, that's gone on to the booking.	Was that all correct? It was …

 In order to check your detailed comprehension of the information given by Grace, listen again and complete the following:

Grace's date of birth:	
Katie's date of birth:	
Grace's surname:	
Katie's surname:	
Credit card number:	
Expiry date:	
Last three digits:	
Booking reference:	
Departure date and time:	
Hotel in Orlando:	
Departure date/time from Orlando:	
Hotel in Cancun:	
Departure date/time from Cancun:	
Total cost of the holiday:	

Chloe uses the standard telephone alphabet to ensure that she spells her client's name correctly. Check online to familiarize yourself with this alphabet and practise saying and understanding it.

A for Alpha, B for Bertie (or sometimes Bravo), C for Charlie, D for Delta …

COBUILD CHECK: credit card language

- We will need your card number and its **expiry date**.
- You must take all reasonable steps to prevent **fraudulent use** of your card.
- There is a magnetic strip on **the back of the card**.
- You should never disclose your **PIN number** to anyone.
- Card details were secure because only **the last four digits** of cards were shown.

C   Changing a booking

1 In this recording, Grace calls Jade in Virgin Customer Services. Listen to the recording. What is the key change Grace wants to make? Will this be possible?

2 Listen to the recording again to check your understanding of the language which the speakers actually use. Complete the phrases.

1 I .... if I could make a change.

2 [...] can I .... and your postcode please?

3 Which part of the holiday .... for?

4 'Cos I can see .... at half past eight in the morning.

5 I think six .... be a good time.

6 It's only an .... anyways.

Note the colloquial use of 'anyways' rather than the standard form 'anyway'.

Clear usage: asking polite questions using past forms

Grace says 'I was just wondering if I could make a small change.'

Past forms are quite often used to make a question more polite, particularly by native speakers, even though they do not refer to the past. Sometimes a more direct question will be clearer for the listener: *Could I make a small change?* or *I'd like to make a small change.* Look back over the transcript for parts A and B in this unit to find other examples of polite questions using past forms such as:

I wanted to check the dates = I want to check the dates/I'd like to check the dates
I was wondering if you could help = I wonder if you could help
Did you mean 6 o'clock? = Do you mean 6 o'clock?

---

3 Put words from the box into the busy or relaxed column.

hustle and bustle	unhurried	noisy	hectic	action-packed	restful
peaceful	lazy	crowded	laid-back	tranquil	full-on

busy	relaxed

Next steps

Have your holiday bookings normally gone as smoothly as Grace's? If you would like to hear further extracts from Grace's conversations, go to **www.collinselt.com/englishforlife/extras**.

6 TECHNICAL HELP

In this unit

1 A Scottish caller asks TalkTalk for help with his broadband connection.

2 A customer takes her phone in for repair in a mobile phone shop.

13

A Assistance with a broken internet connection

Jay calls Liz, who is from near Manchester in north west England. Are you familiar with the internet-related words below? Check their meanings at **www.collinsdictionary.com/cobuild.** Then listen to the recording. If you were the caller, would you be happy with the way Liz helps to solve the broadband problem?

Useful vocabulary and phrases: Internet and broadband	
the router	lower-case / upper-case
DSL	upstream
ADSL	downstream
an ethernet cable	the exchange
the address bar	the browser
authentication	username
generic	password

Liz is very careful to explain technical terms clearly which Jay may not understand. Listen to the recording again and write down the technical terms she uses. Refer to the vocabulary box above as necessary.

1 the 'main kit' you plug into your telephone line. ...*the router (the box with the lights)*...

2 The information which confirms that you are getting on to the Internet. ....

3 The name of the cable that runs between the router and the laptop. ....

4 The field at the top of the browser page. ....

5 The name of the page on the screen where there are three circles (DSL, Internet, wireless). ....

6 The colours currently showing for

   a the wireless light ....

   b the internet light ....

3 Listen again and this time complete the gaps in the phrases which Liz uses to ensure that Jay is following what she is saying.

1 And can I .... who I'm speaking to?

2 [...] from your telephone line your telephone plugged in and .... a router.

3 I'd like you to .... what lights you've got on.

4 So .... is that the signal between ...

5 Now don't worry, I'm .... that.

6 What I ...., is there a cable...?

7 Do you know .... by the address bar?

8 So in the username, I .... all lower case.

9 Um, what .... at the moment, from the information ...

10 Now, ... home telephone number ...?

Liz uses simple non-technical language to keep Jay's attention.' Note some of the phrases she uses:

'I want you to delete/type/enter ...'   'You should see a green light.'

'Can you just repeat that?'   'It says ...'

'A green light should be showing.'   'It shows ...'

Clear usage: non-standard grammar forms

Both speakers use forms of grammar which you will not find in standard English textbooks. Here are some expressions used in the conversation and their standard equivalents:

I've bought a phone here a couple of months ago. =
I bought a phone here a couple of months ago.

Basically, you have issue with your screen. = Basically, you have an issue with your screen.

Do you bought it? = Did you buy it?

So, I can book in for repair? = So I can book it in for repair?

You can come and collect here. = You can come and collect it here.

Did you like to go ahead? = Would you like to go ahead?

---

4 Which words and phrases used by the speakers have similar meanings to the following? First listen to the recording, then refer to the transcript if you need to.

1 Can you let me have your home telephone number, please?

2 I've got some problems with my broadband.

3 Just tell me what is written underneath.

4 Wait a moment. I'll switch off my Wi-Fi.

5 I'll get that ethernet cable.

6 So what should I do now?

7 I've deleted that.

8 I'd like you to type in all small letters, admin.

9 What you should be able to see at the moment ... is that ...

14

B   ## Assistance with a broken phone

Megan, who is originally from Cumbria in the north west of England, takes her mobile phone in for repair at a London branch of Carphone Warehouse. She is helped by Nixon, who is from London. Listen to the recording. Focus on understanding the key information.

1 Write down what the problem is.

....

2 Write down how it can be fixed.

....

So give us a minute = So let me have a minute to think about it

Happy to go with that? = Is that what you would like to do?

 Read through the questions and statements below. Then listen and tick the statements and questions which you hear. All can be used for providing and checking information.

1 Do you have your mobile with you now? ☐

2 Do you have insurance on the phone? ☐

3 We can repair it in the shop. ☐

4 Your mobile has already been booked in for repair ☐

5 I'll update your details on the system. ☐

6 Would you please sign for it? ☐

7 Do you want to put the sim card in yourself? ☐

8 So that's the temporary phone for you. ☐

COBUILD CHECK: repair

- First on his list of priorities is to replace his Porsche which was damaged **beyond repair** in the accident.
- A restorer said that the instrument was damaged but **reparable**.
- He had to bring the boat to a standstill and carry out **temporary repairs**, which fortunately seem to be holding out.
- Check over soft furnishings regularly and **mend** any small holes or tears as they occur before they turn into a major problem.
- The 400-year-old building was **restored** by local craftsmen, and can be hired for wedding receptions.
- Did you **get** the car **fixed**?
- We couldn't afford to do all the work needed to **renovate** the house, so we did the garden instead.

Listening tip: indicating that you understand

Nixon and Megan show that they understand each other by their frequent use of terms such as *'Okay'*, *'Yeah'*, *'That's great'*, *'Thanks'* and *'Right'* throughout the dialogue.

Note also how Nixon repeats what Megan says to confirm a point is clearly understood.
Megan: 'No, I don't have insurance.'
Nixon: 'You don't have insurance.'

When you do not understand information, use questions such as:
Sorry, I didn't follow that/I didn't catch that.
Could you say that again, please?
How does a warranty differ from a guarantee?
Did you say 'mouse'?
(Megan uses the word *'mouse'* when referring to the *'cursor'* on the phone).

3 For detailed practice in understanding the speakers' accents, listen again, pausing the recording as necessary, and complete what they say.

1 Okay, that's fine. Let .... up here.

2 So when the phone .... the repair centre.

3 It's .... the warranty.

4 Um, so your mobile .... for repair.

5 Um, will I get a temporary phone ....?

6 Your new phone has .... so everything (is) ready to go.

Clear usage: first and zero conditional forms

Note the use of the 'first conditional' to explain what *will happen* if a certain action *takes place*.

Megan: 'If *I press* one area, the (mouse'll) mouse *will come up* on another bit.'
'If *you bring it back* next week, *I'll give you* your new phone.'
'If *I pay* for the phone today, *will you give* me a discount?'

And note the use of the 'zero conditional' to indicate what *always happens* when certain actions *take place*.

Nixon: 'If *you fail to* bring it back, *we charge* you.' (Nixon is focusing on 'company policy' – standard procedure if temporary phones are not returned to the store.)

Next steps

How well do you think the speakers in this unit overcame potential communication problems? There are recordings of call-centre phone calls on the Internet which provide further listening-comprehension practice – search for 'Call Centre' (or 'Call Center' *[US]*). If you would like to hear how Liz's conversation with Jay continues, go to **www.collinselt.com/englishforlife/extras.**

7 VOICEMAILS

In this unit

1 This unit features a range of voicemails.

They provide listening comprehension practice but also some useful model language for when you need to leave voicemails in English.

15–18

A Messages: part 1

1 In this section, you will hear five short messages. Focus on the language which frequently recurs as you listen. Listen to the voicemail messages and match them with the reasons for calling.

Voicemail 1		**a**	Confirming a reservation
Voicemail 2		**b**	Going to be late
Voicemail 3		**c**	Where are you?
Voicemail 4		**d**	Booking a table
Voicemail 5		**e**	Have a good holiday!

2 Listen to voicemail 1 again. Do you think Kerry is relaxed or irritated when she leaves her message? Complete the gaps to focus on the language which Kerry uses.

Kerry: Hi there. Um, I'm so sorry .... I'm at the restaurant, it's eight o'clock. I thought we were gonna (going to) meet here round now but you haven't .... , so .... you're running late. If you could just give me a call, let me know, ... uh […] that'd be great. Okay, ... Bye.

3 Listen to voicemail 2. Note how Grace uses 'I *just wanted* to have a chat' in her message. See the 'Clear usage' box. Answer the questions.

1 Where is Clare going next week? ....

2 When will they have a chance to talk? ....

4 In voicemail 3, Katie wants to book a table in a restaurant. Note her use of the past form '*I was wondering* …' to make a polite request. See the 'Clear usage' box and also the one in Unit 5.

1 When is the booking for? ....

2 For how many people? ....

3 What would she like someone from the restaurant to do? ....

Clear usage: 'I just wanted to ask ...'

A polite way to introduce a question or statement is to start a sentence with phrases such as: *I just wanted to ask... .* or *I was wondering if... .* This type of language is often used by native speakers. The past tense is used, but no past meaning is implied.

I just wanted to tell you how much I enjoyed the party.

I wanted to mention that I'll be in Prague at the weekend.

I was wondering if you could let me borrow your car at the weekend.

I was wondering if you are free tomorrow.

5 Make these sentences shorter by deleting some words and changing word forms if necessary.

1 I just wanted to let you know I'm running late.

2 I've been stuck in a traffic jam for half an hour.

3 I'm not very happy about this.

4 It'll be good to talk later.

5 I'm not going to take the motorway next time.

In voicemail 4, note that Mike says 'Just letting you know …' (not: I'm just letting you know) and 'Encountered quite bad traffic' (not: I encountered…). This type of omission (known as 'conversational deletion') occurs in informal spoken language, emails and text messages.

6 Listen to voicemail 5 and answer the questions. Note that 'The Red Lion' mentioned in the message is a pub and restaurant.

1 Is Josh likely to be …
    a the pub landlord   b a customer?

2 Is the table reservation …
    a for outside   b for inside?

3 Is the weather currently …
    a good   b bad?

4 Is the reservation for …
    a tomorrow night   b tomorrow lunchtime?

Useful vocabulary and phrases: starting a voicemail

Hi [Ellie], John here – hope you're well.

… I'm just calling because …

… I'm so sorry I missed you.

… Sorry, I couldn't talk earlier.

… I just wanted to let you know that …

… I'm sorry, but I'm going to be late.

… I'm on my way.

… Can you call me back when you get this?

20–25

B **Messages: part 2**

1 Listen to the voicemail messages and match them with the reasons for calling.

Voicemail	6	**a**	Think I'm lost
Voicemail	7	**b**	I was in a meeting
Voicemail	8	**c**	Left something behind
Voicemail	9	**d**	A delayed flight
Voicemail	10	**e**	Giving directions
Voicemail	11	**f**	Will send some documents

2 Listen to voicemail 6 and complete some of the key information in the message. The speaker, Mirka, is from Slovakia.

1 We were the table of ....

2 I might have left my ....behind.

3 [...] it could be .... or .... or something (somewhere).

4 It's .... with charms.

3 In voicemail 7, Teresa has just missed a call from her Finnish colleague, Virpi. What do you think Teresa says in her voicemail? Complete the gaps first without listening and then listen and compare what you have written with what Teresa actually says.

1 I was just .... my car.

2 Anyway, I .... the update later …

3 I .... some other documents …

4 Anyway give me a ring if .... any questions.

4 In voicemail 8, Katie has missed a call. Complete the phrases she uses by matching words in the columns, then listen to the voicemail to check your answers.

1 I was	**a**	a call back this evening
2 Okay,	**b**	to have a chat
3 We haven't spoken	**c**	in a meeting
4 So give me	**d**	in a while
5 Be good	**e**	lots of love
6 Sorry	**f**	it's Katie
7 Hi,	**g**	to miss your call

Katie says: 'Be good to have a chat' = 'it would be good to have a chat'. As mentioned earlier in this unit, words are often left out in fast, informal speech.
Would be great if you could call me (It would be great if you could call me)
Call you later (I'll call you later)

5 Listen to voicemail 9. The speaker, Layan, is from Sri Lanka. The line is not so clear and his language is not 'standard' English. Which of these two factors might cause you greater listening problems?

1 Answer the questions:

    a Where is Layan now? ....

    b Why is his flight delayed? ....

2 Note what Layan actually says and write the standard English equivalent.

    a my flight been delayed … ....

    b (I will) … keep you update. ....

Useful vocabulary and phrases: returning voicemail messages

Sorry I couldn't speak earlier – I was in a meeting.

I just got/picked up your message.   I'm free now – can you call me back?

Sorry we got cut off.   My battery died.

I don't know what happened earlier.   I didn't have any mobile reception.

---

6 Listen to voicemail 10 in which Eva, who is from Salzburg in Austria, asks for help when she is lost. She is on her way to view a house which she is interested in renting. Complete the phrases.

1 I'm .... to view your house.

2 I'm on my way but think I'm .... lost.

3 I'm..................... if I'm on the right road.

4 If you..................... me a ring back that .... great.

7 In voicemail 11 James, who is from London, leaves some directions for a friend. Listen out for the phrases which he uses and check that you would know where to go by answering the questions.

If you just follow the road   Follow it along until you can see …

You'll come to …   We're just in front of you

1 What will his friend come to if she follows the road?

2 Then how far is it before she sees the bridge?

3 Does she need to cross the river?

Next steps

This unit contains a range of everyday voicemail messages. Are there any messages which you often leave which have not been included? Refer to the transcripts and use the phrases in the recordings to practise leaving messages of your own. Go to **www.collinselt.com/englishforlife/extras** where you will find some more voicemails and transcripts.

8 REGISTRATION AND INDUCTION

In this unit

1 A Polish facilities manager gives an 'induction' tour to a new employee.

2 An administrator in a UK doctor's surgery registers a new patient.

A Induction to a new workplace: part 1

26

1 How would you introduce where you work or study to some new employees or students? Before you listen to the recording, check that you understand the words and phrases below. Then listen to the recording and compare what Karolina says with what you might say. Consider the strategies you use for checking information and questions you would ask.

Useful vocabulary and phrases: workplace inductions		
induction	fire marshals	sculpt
ATM	evacuation exercise	squash
flickering light	hospitality manager	

2 Listen again to the first part of the recording (up to the point where Karolina talks about their 'current location'). Note down the details below.

1 Opening times Monday to Friday? ....

2 Opening times on Saturday, Sunday, Bank Holidays? ....

3 How many floors are there? ....

4 How many 'areas' are there on each floor? ....

5 What is their current location? ....

Karolina uses informal English. Note the more formal equivalents of what she says:

Informal	More formal
'You can just give Carl a buzz.'	*You can call Carl. / You can ring Carl.*
'We're done here.'	*We have finished here.*
'to order stuff'	*to order things*

3 Now listen to the recording from where you have paused it. Concentrate on what Karolina says about the kitchen, fire regulations, sports facilities and café. Answer these questions.

1   Where are the kitchens located? ....

2   How often do fire evacuations take place? ....

3   Where are the squash courts? ....

4   What other classes are available to staff? ....

5   When is the café open? ....

6   Where is the ATM? ....

7   What is the name of the hospitality manager? ....

B Induction to a new workplace: part 2

1 Karolina talks about the post room, the main reception and the facilities department, as well as providing some information about security passes. Listen to the recording. Make notes about what you consider to be the most important information for a new starter in the company.

27

Clear usage: passive forms

Karolina switches between using informal language and more formal language when she is describing specific office procedures. Note these examples where the use of the passive form emphasizes standard office practice.'

'Everything that's over 100 pages *should be sent* to the reprographics room.'

'If you need your documents *to be bound* ...'

'The post room *can be contacted* ...'

'Every person needs *to have their photo taken.*'

---

2 Now play the recording again. Are these statements true or false? Do the statements focus on the information which you considered to be most important when you first listened?

		True	False
1	There are four internal mail collections per day.	....	....
2	The courier service is not available after 5.30 p.m.	....	....
3	People doing work experience do not receive security passes.	....	....
4	The company has showers which employees can use.	....	....
5	[...] but they need to bring their own towels.	....	....
6	Anna is responsible for parking requests.	....	....
7	Mauricio is available in the office today.	....	....
8	If employees change jobs, the Facilities Helpdesk is informed automatically.	....	....
9	The first-aid room is located next to the facilities office.	....	....

3 With reference to what you heard in the recording, match the verbs with the word or phrase. More than one answer is possible, but try to remember the word combinations which you heard.

1	to sign up for	**a**	the accident book
2	to update	**b**	security passes
3	to fill in	**c**	the system
4	to take	**d**	the switchboard operators
5	to inform	**e**	a shower
6	to issue	**f**	classes

C Registering with a doctor

Jo, the administrator, is from Bristol in the west of England. The new patient, Yasmeen, is originally from Kenya, but she has lived in the UK for many years.

Read through the notes below and then listen to the recording to familiarize yourself with the speakers' accents. Note, for example, Jo's rising intonation even when she makes statements. This is typical of a Bristol accent. Some details have been omitted from the recording for confidentiality purposes.

> Jo responds positively and with encouragement to Yasmeen using words like 'lovely' and 'wonderful'. Although common, such words are not used frequently by all British speakers of English. Jo also uses 'OK',' Alright', 'Yes' and 'Yeah' frequently to maintain a high level of interaction.

Useful vocabulary and phrases: registering at a health centre

GP = General Practitioner (a doctor who works in 'primary care'). In the UK, most patients first go to a GP who will refer them to a hospital specialist if necessary.

a GP practice = a group of GPs which is responsible for a specific area. Normally you can only register for a practice if you are within a practice 'boundary'.

a utility bill = a bill from a utility company. The utility companies are, for example, electricity, telephone and water suppliers.

a postcode = a zipcode [US]

Rochdale = a town in the North of England

---

2 Listen to the recording again. Complete the questions (and statements) which Jo uses to obtain information. Stop the recording when you reach statement 10.

1 Now, I understand .... our GP practice.

2 First of all can I check that .... in our practice boundary.

3 And can I ask ...., please?

4 Now I need you .... live.

5 So I understand .... there.

6 and I also understand .... bill.

7 Do you mind awfully .... it?

8 Would you like me .... you?

9 Could you .... for me?

10 So if you'd .... for me?

Clear usage: 'colloquial' expressions

Jo and Yasmeen use some everyday UK-specific colloquial expressions such as:

'Do you mind awfully?' = *Do you mind very much?* (very polite!)

Do you mind me asking awfully? Do you really, really mind? (extremely polite!!}

'If you could complete that for me, please' = *Please complete that.*

'Okay, if you'd like to pop that on there?' = *Could you write that down?*

'Cos' = *Because*   'There we go' = *That's it, that's done.*

 Can you answer these questions from memory? Listen to the recording one more time to check your answers.

1 How does Jo check that the patient's address is within the practice boundary?

2 Does the patient have a bank statement with her?

3 For how long did Yasmeen live in Rochdale?

4 Where was she born?

5 What does Yasmeen need to provide at the bottom of the form?

6 Does she have any drug allergies?

7 How long has she suffered from high blood pressure?

8 How long will it take before registration is finalized?

Note that Yasmeen says 'I born there' instead of the standard form, 'I was born there'.

COBUILD CHECK: register

- This illness occurred within a week of moving and I had not **registered with** a local doctor.
- To **register for** the conference please complete the form and return it with payment.
- To register for the seminar, **complete** the **registration form** and send it to this address.
- When firms register with the FDA they are given a **registration number**.

Next steps

The accents in this recording may not be familiar to you, but they show the wide range of English which you will meet in a world where most people do not speak with standard British or American accents. Focus on understanding accents which you meet most frequently and for unexpected pronunciation and intonation.

9 GETTING ALONG

In this unit

1 Two male friends, both from the UK, talk about their former and present housemates.

2 Two female friends, also from the UK, talk about how they get on with their husbands.

A Living with housemates

29

 1 Listen to the recording and write down the issues which John and Freddy say can become a problem in a shared flat. John speaks first.

2 Listen again. Circle the correct word to complete each of the phrases the speaker uses.

1 John and Freddy say that their brothers are both *easy/difficult* to live with.

2 John *argues/doesn't argue* with his brother.

3 Freddy is *looking forward to/not looking forward to* living with his old university friends.

4 Freddy *was happy/refused* to clear up other people's mess in his university flat.

5 John's university housemate *did all the cleaning/shared cleaning duties with John.*

COBUILD CHECK: tolerate

• This is my home, I won't **tolerate** such rudeness.

• He became quite **intolerant of** people who he thought were ignorant.

• She understood him and above all else was **tolerant of** his quirks.

• These were the little pleasures that made a hard life **tolerable**.

• His grovelling manner was **intolerable** at times.

3 Read through the phrases which occur in the recording. Then listen and put them in the order in which they are said. If you are not familiar with the phrases, try to understand the meaning from the context. Then check them in a dictionary or **www.collinsdictionary.com/cobuild**.

1 […] because you've had the same upbringing. ☐

2 […] they've become firm friends … ☐

3 There's more room for disagreeing on how you should live. ☐

4 I think people might argue with their siblings. ☐

5 […] we didn't clash. ☐

6 […] he had been holding a grudge against me. ☐

7 The trick is to find other grumpy people! ☐

8 We're all sticklers for principle. ☐

9 I'm fairly intolerant of people's feelings. ☐

Clear usage: past perfect continuous

When talking about his former housemates, John says 'I found out at the end of the year that he had been holding a grudge against me'.

Note the contrast between the past perfect continuous (*he had been holding a grudge*) and the simple past (*I found out*).

John *found out* at a later date that during all the time *he had been living* with his flatmate, his flatmate *had been holding a grudge* against him.
He said he *had been cleaning up* after me.
He *had been washing up* my dishes.
He *had been putting up* with all the noise I made/*had been making* for more than a year!

---

4 Complete the phrases by matching a verb with the words.

1	to tidy up	**a**	the same TV shows
2	to do	**b**	someone mad
3	to watch	**c**	that we take our shoes off
4	to hold/bear	**d**	all the cleaning
5	to drive	**e**	a stray cat into the house
6	to let	**f**	someone else's mess
7	to insist	**g**	a grudge against someone

5 Choose words from the box which are you consider to be related to 'tolerant' and 'intolerant' behaviour.

easy-going	unaccepting	accepting	prejudiced
understanding	unprejudiced	biased	forbearing
sympathetic	bigoted	laid-back	disapproving

tolerant	intolerant

B What makes a relationship work?

30

① Listen to the recording, in which Karen speaks first. How compatible or incompatible are Celia and Karen with their husbands?

1 regarding money

2 regarding driving

② Test your general understanding by answering these questions, but don't worry if you do not understand every word. There will be a chance to check any new vocabulary later.

1 Where did Celia meet Pete?
2 Does Celia's husband Pete write a lot of poetry?
3 What does Celia find particularly attractive about Pete?
4 In which area does Karen think that being compatible is most important?
5 Which area does Celia identify as one that can make things difficult in a relationship?
6 Where does Karen have her biggest arguments with her husband?
7 Who would be the worst backseat driver, Pete or Andy?
8 What does Karen find particularly annoying about her husband when he is driving?

Clear usage: speculation

Celia says: 'I imagine that if I ever drove, then I'd have the worst backseat driver next to me.'

In this case Celia *uses* the '2nd conditional' to speculate about what *would happen* if she *drove*. Note that *'were to'* can also be used instead of the simple past tense.

He **would** be very upset if **I damaged/I were to damage** his car.
No-one **would believe** it if **I started/I were to start** piano lessons.
I know she **would be** angry with me if **I drove/I were to drive** her car without her permission.

③ Note the words which Karen and Celia use and, if necessary, check meanings in a dictionary or **www.collinsdictionary.com/cobuild**. Select the words to complete the sentences below. The words in brackets are synonyms.

creative	swerving	compatible	rows	curious
pull (him) up	outset	backseat driver	blokes *(slang)*	cautious

1 He's very .... and I admire that in him. (imaginative)
2 I always .... on this. (correct)
3 At the .... of a relationship you think you know the things that are gonna be important. (beginning)
4 Are you two quite .... in terms of your attitude to money? (well-matched)
5 We're both quite ...., but he's more generous than I am. (careful)
6 We have our biggest .... in the car. (arguments)
7 We ended up .... all over these eight lane motorways. (moving from side to side)
8 I imagine that if I ever drove, I'd have the worst .... next to me. (an annoying passenger)

Listening tip: interacting sympathetically

Note the phrases which Karen and Celia use that make the conversation flow and which maintain interaction. Note particularly how they refer to shared past experience and respond sympathetically to new information.

'*You're sure* he actually wrote it?'

'And that's something that you found attractive in him?'

'And so *what about you* and Andy?'

'You're more generous than Andy?'

'*Oh really?*'

'*So* you're navigating or you're driving.'

'*Oh really, as well as* driving?'

4 Make the following questions and statements more interactive by adding phrases from the box.

hasn't it	don't we	isn't it true that	won't you
can't you	weren't we	didn't we	tell me
don't you	isn't it	don't you think	can't we

1 We like going for long drives, ... ?

2 .... you lived in a house with eight other people when you were a student?

3 .... what it was like when you first met Chris.

4 You can remember that day well, ... ?

5 You'll be going to the World Cup, ... ?

6 It has been a really enjoyable day, ... ?

7 So .... have a good time yesterday!

8 We were going to arrange a birthday party for Asim, ... ?

9 It is a beautiful day today, ...

10 We can arrange another date for the party, ...

11 You remember meeting Jacki, ...

12 So .... we should try and sort things out.

Next steps

Reflect on how you listen and try to understand a speaker when you do not understand all of the words which they use. Focus on trying to understand from the context. Try to understand the 'gist' of what is said without worrying about understanding the exact meaning of every word. To hear more of Karen and Celia's conversation, go to **www.collinselt.com/englishforlife/extras** and focus on how they interact to ensure that the conversation flows.

10 CULTURAL OBSERVATIONS

In this unit

1 Cultural observations from an American–German couple who have recently moved to Germany.

2 Hussain from Saudi Arabia compares his experience of family life and studying in Saudi Arabia and the UK.

A An American–German marriage

31

1 Lauren and Dieter, who are from Michigan in the USA and Aachen in Germany, are now living in Munich, Germany. Listen to the recording and summarize what the speakers say about:

- the similarities between life in New York and Munich. (Lauren)
- feelings about 'cross-cultural' relationships. (Dieter)

2 Listen again to check you understand the details and decide whether the following sentences are true or false.

		True	False
1	Lauren and Dieter found that moving to Germany from England was easier than a move from America to Germany would have been.	....	....
2	Lauren believes that some 'rituals' in Germany are closer to 'rituals' in England than 'rituals' in America.	....	....
3	According to Lauren, everyone goes for Sunday lunch in England.	....	....
4	Lauren had not expected there to be so many differences between life in New York and life in Munich.	....	....
5	Cross-cultural relationships are easy according to Dieter.	....	....
6	The couple are suffering from 'logistical headaches'.	....	....

COBUILD CHECK: shared culture and cultural differences

- Companies are losing international business because they lack language skills and **cultural awareness**.
- I had never been to Australia before so I was in for a huge **culture shock**.
- A nation is based on **shared culture** and traditions.
- The film observes the **culture clash** between immigrants and their Americanized children.
- Any debate about **multiculturalism** should give consideration to our history as a country of migrants.
- The US has become more of a **multicultural** society than ever before.

Clear usage: modal verbs referring to the past

Lauren and Dieter have recently moved to Germany directly from the UK (not from the USA). They say that the move was easier than it *would have been* if they had moved directly from the States. (The fact that it was easier to move to Germany from the UK was probably a matter of the proximity of the two countries, given the fact that they think that life in Germany and the USA is more similar).

Other uses of modal verbs used to comment on past events or actions.

*It **would have** been difficult.* (it was actually very easy)

*You **might have** called me.* (You didn't call me)

*They **should have** let us know.* (They didn't let us know)

*I don't think we **could have** done things differently.* (We did everything as well as we could)

*We **needn't have** rushed.* (The meeting hadn't started when we arrived)

B   A Saudi Arabian living in the UK

32

1 Hussain is from Abha in the south west of Saudi Arabia. Listen to the recording and then summarize the comparisons which he makes between family life and study in Saudi Arabia and the UK. Are there any parts of the recording which you find difficult to understand? Is this because of the speed at which Hussain speaks, his accent, his use of vocabulary?

2 Listen to the recording again. Tick the statements which best represent Hussain's views.

1   Relationships between family members are normally good in the UK. ☐

2   He does not approve of "houses for the elderly". (special accommodation for older people) ☐

3   It's not that she has to cover everything. ☐

4   In most cases, he believes there is greater support from the family for older people in Saudi Arabia. ☐

5   In most cases, men and women do not mix in Saudi Arabia. ☐

6   If she prefers, she may go for colours. ☐

7   Some schools and universities are co-educational in Saudi Arabia. ☐

8   He adapted easily to a co-educational class when he studied in the UK. ☐

9   He believes he needs to learn to communicate with both male and female students in order to learn English well. ☐

Clear usage: expressing tentative opinions

Hussain is careful to qualify his statements. He is not dogmatic, but gives opinions from his experience whilst acknowledging that there may be other views.

'In many cases, …'

'It's slightly different, …'

'From what I have seen, …'

'You would normally see …'

'As you can imagine, …'

3 Listen again, and identify words and phrases in the recording which have the same meanings as those below.

   1 a duty ....

   2 to visit ....

   3 what is usual and expected ....

   4 older people ....

   5 keeping people apart ....

   6 attitudes and way of thinking ....

   7 education intended for both males and females ....

   8 to meet ....

4 Hussain speaks English clearly, but some aspects of his pronunciation may cause difficulties if you are not familiar with his accent. Listen to the recording again whilst reading the transcript. Underline the words which you did not understand when you listened for the first time.

C   Adapting to a different dress code

33

1 Hussain goes on to focus on dress codes for visitors to Saudi Arabia and also gives advice to Saudi women visiting the UK. Before you listen, think about what advice he might give. Listen to the recording and compare your predictions with what he actually says.

2 Focus on Hussain's pronunciation of specific words and phrases by completing the following sentences. Start and stop the recording as necessary.

   1 Um, for example, if she is a lady, she should expect there is .... or for the dress.

   2 We call this in Saudi Arabia ....

   3 Um, otherwise she will have .... the, maybe the— from the legal perspective.

   4 Uh, ... for a lady coming from Saudi Arabia ...

   5 [...] she has to bear in mind that the black colour is not common ....
      to wear [it].

   6 And maybe ...., she may go for some of the light colours.

COBUILD CHECK: dress code

- She bathed her baby and dressed him in clean **clothes**.
- When working outside wear warm **clothing** that allows full mobility of the arms and legs.
- They say their prayers in the prayer hall and **wear traditional** Muslim **dress**.
- Guests at Bangazai Lodge wore **formal dress** for dinner and Benjamin's jeans stood out.
- There has been a trend towards more **casual dress** in the workplace.
- It was 90 degrees in the heat and Jones was **over-dressed** in a suit.
- Most of the women were **well dressed** – in expensive silk if they could afford it.
- He was always dirty and **badly dressed**.
- He had a wicked sense of humour and great **dress sense**.

Clear usage: modals with infinitive form

Hussain uses the passive infinitive form with *'might'*. Note that the infinitive is used without 'to' after modal verbs (except 'ought to').

'She *might be advised* to wear the abaya.'
'She *may be asked* to change her clothes.'
'We *should be told* about this beforehand.'
'It *ought to be* clearly *stated* in the travel guides.'
'We *must be made* aware of the law.'

3 Hussain has an advanced level of English and works in English on a daily basis but he uses some non-standard forms. Write down a 'standard' English equivalent of what he says.

Hussain says	Standard English
there is different attitudes	....
She has to wear a modest dress	....
certain type of clothing	....
by police	....
the opposite way	....
she has to bear in mind that	....

4 Rewrite these sentences in the passive.

1 We ought to tell them about the dress code.
They ought to be told about the dress code.

2 The travel agent should give you information about local customs.
You ....

3 They might ask you to take your shoes off.
You ....

4 'Your tour guide must offer you the opportunity to ask questions.'
You ....

5 You ought to park your car in a secure area at night.
Your car ....

6 The police may fine you if you drop litter in the streets.
You ....

Next steps

Have you been surprised by anything the speakers have said in this unit? Lauren talks about cultural 'rituals', such as the Sunday lunch in the UK. What cultural rituals would you identify in your country? If you work with Arabic speakers of English, seek out recordings on the Internet.

11 SOCIAL MEDIA

In this unit

1 British and American friends compare their views on social networking.

2 Alison, from the north of England, explains why she does not approve of social networking.

34

A The pros and cons of Twitter™

1 Consider your own arguments for and against the use of social media sites. Then listen to the recording. Compare your thoughts about the use of social media with what Dan and Lily say.

2 To test your recognition of the language Dan and Lily use, listen again and complete the sentences and phrases.

1 […] but I find it difficult .... with my own life, let alone spending lots of time .... what I believe to be relevant information.

2 I tend to think that the use of websites like Twitter has reduced .... that people have.

3 Well, like .... and .... on Twitter are essential the same thing.

4 Is Brad Pitt going to .... about Angelina Jolie?

5 It's definitely ...., communicating ....

6 If I'm sitting on the train and .... favourite game, …

7 […] then I guess .... to things like Twitter to try and keep up to date.

8 […] but then it .... personal preference and enjoyment.

Clear usage: non-standard use of conditionals

Note that Dan and Lily, in common with many native English speakers, do not stick to 'standard' rules concerning their use of conditional forms.

Lily: 'If you were someone with loads of followers, you have to …'

Lily: 'How often would you check your phone, the,

Dan: 'When I have nothing else to do.'

Standard grammar rules suggest that other forms might be used, such as:

Lily: *If you were someone with loads of followers, you **would have to**.*

Lily: *How often would you check your phone, then?* Dan: *When **I had** nothing else to do.*

or *How often/When do you check your phone, then?* Dan: *When **I have** nothing else to do.*

The 'rules' for English conditional forms as taught in schools around the world are often broken by native and non-native speakers in everyday speech.

3 Which is the standard conditional form in these sentences? Tick a or b.

1 a Would you spend more time on Facebook™ if you aren't so busy? ☐

b Would you spend more time on Facebook if you weren't so busy? ☐

2 a If I had more time, I would learn Korean. ☐

b If I have more time, I would learn Korean. ☐

3 a If I hear from Chris this afternoon, I'll call you. ☐

b If I'll hear from Chris this afternoon, I'll call you. ☐

4 a Would you answer your phone if it would ring during a meeting? ☐

b Would you answer your phone if it rang during a meeting? ☐

Listening tip: unfinished sentences

As is the case with many speakers, Dan and Lily do not always complete their sentences. They start a sentence, stop and then perhaps move off in another direction. Here are some examples – check the transcripts for others.

'Twitter is just a different, it's the same, it's the same type of stuff.'

'What, what, how often would you check your phone then?'

'I'd watch the telly though, I'd switch to the telly, if I had a telly.' telly = television [UK slang]

B **The future of social media**

1 David from Los Angeles and Larry from New Jersey consider the importance of sites such as Facebook, Twitter and LinkedIn. Listen to the recording. Do you use the sites mentioned? Do you use other sites? Perhaps you are not interested in 'social networking'? Compare your views with those of the speakers.

35

2 Complete the grid based on the nouns and/or adjectives used by the speakers.

Noun	Adjective
obsession	obsessed
selection	
	fun
	obliged
disadvantage	
spontaneity	
	strong

David and Larry's phone call is challenging to understand because the quality of the connection is, at times, bad. When dealing with a bad connection like this, it is important to listen for key words – from these, more often than not you will be able to decipher the meaning of the whole phrase.

Listen to the recording again. Tick the expressions which the speakers use. Which of the statements do you agree or disagree with?

1   […] I don't care what other people who I barely know are doing, … ☐
2   I go on my son's Facebook page every once in a while. ☐
3   I am obsessed and waste too much time. ☐
4   I agree about the wasting time aspect. ☐
5   The quality of posts on Facebook tends to be high. ☐
6   […] most people now find social media an obligation rather than fun. ☐
7   […] if I'm not on Twitter, I'm at a disadvantage … ☐
8   It's not going to lose its spontaneous appeal. ☐

COBUILD CHECK: social media

• The service allows you to **upload** images and video.
• Do not post rude or abusive **messages**, including personal attacks on other users.
• He was banned from the website after **trolling** persistently.
• The site is controlled by a **moderator** so there will be a slight delay before you can view your message.
• The company's open-access forum received **traffic** of up to 10,000 users every day until it was shut down last year.
• His **posts** are entertaining and informative – he's a favourite among visitors to our website.

4   Match the phrases with the definitions.

1   lose its appeal   a   have the same problems as others
2   be in the same boat   b   not be so popular
3   cross a line   c   watch secretly
4   spy on   d   not to take part
5   confess   e   do something that you shouldn't
6   miss out on   f   admit to others

C   Different attitudes to using social media

1   Rachael is from Newcastle in the north east of England and Alison comes from the county of Cumbria in the north west. Listen to the recording and particularly note how Alison expresses her scepticism about social media. Do you share Rachael's views or Alison's?

The Lake District – a beautiful area of England in the north west of the country.
Cheerios™ – a popular breakfast cereal
bragging (to brag) – to boast, to speak in an arrogant way

2 Now listen again and then answer the questions to test your detailed comprehension.

1 What does Rachael have displayed on her Twitter page?

2 What kind of boring information do some people tweet about?

3 How does Rachael describe what a lot of people write in their Facebook updates?

4 What kind of people does Rachael mainly 'follow' on Twitter?

5 What kind of 'Tweets' does Rachael mainly send?

6 How many 'followers' does she have?

3 Note the language of disapproval which Alison uses in the box below. Did you write down these expressions when listening to the recording for the first time?

Clear usage: disapproval

Alison strongly disapproves of social media. Her exaggerated expressions and rhetorical questions make her opinions very clear to the listener:

'It's just really boring, mundane stuff.'

'I mean, who wants to know all that?'

'Well, I think it's all bragging!'

'Is your phone not always buzzing?'

'If everyone's constantly tweeting and retweeting and everything else, surely ...'

---

4 Alison listens actively to what Rachael is saying by regularly interjecting with 'yeah, yeah', 'Aww!', 'Okay', 'Oh' etc. Listen to the recording and complete the other phrases she uses to encourage Rachael to say more.

1 But, 'cos .... a lot of these people ...

2 I mean, who .... all that?

3 Do they .... too?

4 Well, I think .... bragging!

5 Is your phone .... buzzing?

6 Do you not find .... over?

Next steps

Which of the speakers in this unit do you tend to agree with most? How has the use of social media developed since this recording was made? If you would like to hear more from Rachael and Alison, go to **www.collinselt.com/englishforlife/extras**. You will also find more from Dan and Lily, who feature in the first recording.

---

12 ATTITUDES TO WORK

In this unit

1 Two friends, both from the UK, discuss their experience of living and working in Hong Kong, Sweden and Singapore.

2 An Austrian currently working in London, compares her experience of living and working in Austria and in the UK.

37

A **Striking the right work-life balance**

Listen to the recording and note down what the speakers feel about their work-life balance in the different countries they have lived in. If you have lived in these countries, have you had similar experiences?

COBUILD CHECK: work pressures

- He worked long hours at a **stressful** job and rarely exercised.
- Some of the keys to good health are a good diet and a **stress-free**, intellectually rewarding job.
- I was in a very mentally **demanding** job doing computer programming.
- People want a job which is creative and **challenging**.
- Employees need the right resources to do the job and a good **working environment**.
- **Heavy workloads** and pressure to meet targets were said to be the main spark for stress-related illnesses.
- A recruiter might be advertizing your **dream** job online right now!

2 Listen to the recording again. Check your comprehension by indicating whether these statements are true or false.

		True	False
1	Karen approves of the work-life balance in Sweden.	....	....
2	Celia did not like the fact that working hours in Sweden were longer in the winter.	....	....
3	In Hong Kong, life was very hectic.	....	....
4	Karen was able to spend more time at home when she lived in Singapore.	....	....
5	Karen found the travelling part of her work very tiring.	....	....
6	Karen worked so hard when her daughter was very young that she believes she missed out on her daughter's early development.	....	....

Clear usage: 'would' to express habits in the past

Note what Karen says about the time she spent in Hong Kong (when she was 'young') and what she says about when she worked in Singapore.

'We'd generally go out and party till 3a.m.'
'I would try to be home by 6.30.'

In both cases, she uses *would* to refer to what she did repeatedly in the past. Compare this common use of *would* with *used to*, which is also used to talk about past habits. *Used to* is more flexible and can refer to past situations (not only habits).

We used to go out a lot. / *We would go out a lot.* (when we lived in Hong Kong)
I used to live in Hong Kong. ~~I would live in Hong Kong.~~ (a situation and not a habit, so *would* is not used)

3 Tick the sentences where 'used to' and 'would' are used correctly when referring to what happened in the past. Sometimes, both options are correct.

1 a When I lived in Finland I used to cycle to work every day. ☐

 b When I lived in Finland I would cycle to work every day. ☐

2 a Did you use to own a Mercedes when you lived in Germany? ☐

 b Would you own a Mercedes when you lived in Germany? ☐

3 a Didn't you use to sing in a choir? ☐

 b Wouldn't you sing in a choir? ☐

4 a I used to spend an hour playing computer games when I got home. ☐

 b I would spend an hour playing computer games when I got home. ☐

4 Indicate whether these words used in the recording are negative or positive. Check the transcript to see how the speakers use these words and how frequently they use them.

| flexible | tough | disillusioned | exhausting |
| glamorous | wearing | unsettling | fabulous |

Negative	Frequency	Positive	Frequency

Celia and Karen employ lots of 'active listening' techniques in their conversation. This means that they make it clear to the other person that they are listening carefully by mirroring what the other says, finishing each other's sentences, and making noises like 'Mmm' and 'Yeah' at regular intervals.

5 Listen to the recording again and this time focus on how Celia empathizes with and checks her understanding of what Karen tells her. Write down what Celia says in response to Karen's comments. Note that sentences are not always finished.

1 And I think as a society they had a pretty good balance of work and leisure. *In Sweden?*

2 Goodness, I worked six day a week.

....

3 [...] so I was away for up to two weeks at a time.

....

4 [...] and I became pretty disillusioned with it by the end and just wanted to be at home.

....

5 [...] and then you're away for another week.

....

6 To do that for two or three years is – when you've got a young family as well.

....

B ## Comparing working life in the UK and Austria

38

1 Listen to the recording in which Eva, who is from Salzburg in Austria, compares living and working in Austria with working in London. What does she say about:

● working in London? ....
● working in Austria? ....

2 Listen again and answer the following questions to check your comprehension.

1 How did Eva travel to work in Austria?
2 How does she travel to work in London?
3 How long does it take her to get to work in London?
4 What does she like about working life in London?
5 What is Eva's opinion of the attitude towards work in Austria?
6 What is one of the first questions you are asked in London when you meet someone new?

Listening tip: common 'non-standard' use of present tenses

Eva uses many 'standard' forms of the simple present:
'What *I like* about working in the UK is …'
'In Austria *we have* a funny mix …'
'… *people add* that label to you …'

But she also uses the continuous form when 'standard' English usage would suggest using *the simple present:*
'*We're starting* work at, like, nine.' *(We start work at around 9)*
'… and then *you're getting out* of the office a bit earlier.' *(You get out of the office a little earlier)*

You will hear many examples of the continuous form of the present when you might expect to hear the simple form in everyday speech – used by 'native' and 'non-native' speakers.

3 The sentences below focus on the language of comparing attitudes and points of view. Listen again and tick the phrases which Eva uses.

1 […] working in Austria is quite different to working in the UK. ☐
2 […] in the end it made the day a lot longer … ☐
3 However, what I really like about working in the UK … ☐
4 On the other hand, I prefer … ☐
5 […] the attitude is also quite different … ☐
6 So in Austria we have a funny attitude. ☐
7 In comparison, family life is very similar. ☐
8 Whereas working in London […] you identify yourself with what you do … ☐

COBUILD CHECK: work routines

- Avoiding the **daily commute** could greatly enhance the quality of people's lives.
- How does she manage to balance the long **anti-social working hours** of restaurant work with motherhood?
- Offering staff **flexible working hours** helps to reduce absenteeism.
- With self-employment you have greater flexibility – no more commuting or **nine-to-five** routine.
- He does a ten-hour **shift** four days a week.
- Doctors operate out-of-hours **rotas**, meaning that there is a duty psychiatrist available at all times.

4 Can you remember which words used by Eva have the same meaning as the following? Listen to the recording again to check your memory and refer to the transcript if necessary.

1 travel to and from work regularly   ....
2 (a distance) which can be covered on foot   ....
3 (a distance) which can be travelled by bicycle ....
4 the underground or subway   ....
5 a person who gets up early in the morning   ....
6 very important, leading   ....

Next steps

Have you had similar experiences to the speakers in terms of balancing your work-study life with your home life? Are you more of a 'work to live' or a 'live to work' person? Go online to find out about peoples' experiences of living in different countries. 'Work-life balance' may be a good starting point for finding out what people have to say about maintaining a healthy lifestyle.

13 CHARITIES

In this unit

1 A fluent speaker of English originally from Barcelona, talks about her work for Macmillan Cancer Support.

2 A discussion between two British speakers about which charities they support.

39

A   Working for a charity

Inés, who is originally from Barcelona, talks about her work for Macmillan Cancer Support. Listen to the recording. As you listen, consider these questions.

1 Would you take a similar career path to Inés?

2 If so, why? If not, why not?

> **Listening tip:** understanding variations in vowel sounds
>
> There is great variety in the pronunciation of vowel sounds amongst native and non-native speakers of English. We need to practise our understanding of this variety of sounds in order to communicate with people from different parts of the world who have different accents.
>
> Inés is a clear speaker of English, but her pronunciation of words such as 'appreciate', 'need' and 'another' in these examples may be unfamiliar to you.
>
> 'I've got skills that, you know, that they *appreciate*.'
>
> *'We also gave grants to people who need money.'*
>
> 'I remember *another* call that really touched me.'

2 Play the recording again and answer the questions to check your detailed understanding of the recording.

1 What made Inés give up her old job and start work for Macmillan Cancer Support?

2 Why was it such a difficult decision to leave her old job?

3 How did she start working for Macmillan?

4 How does she feel about her current job with the charity?

5 What is Macmillan well-known for?

6 What is the charity less well-known for?

7 She mentions situations where the charity has given money to cancer sufferers – what are they?

8 What was the reason for the donation which she mentions at the end of the recording?

COBUILD CHECK: giving to charity

- Profits from the sale of these prints will go to McCartney's **favourite charity**.
- Paul never charges clients but asks them to **make a donation to charity** instead.
- A woman who secretly played the stock market **left** nearly £2 million **to charity** in her will.
- Look at the website to see how you can get involved in **supporting** the **charity** right now.
- He regularly donates substantial sums of money to **local charities**.
- Give away toys or clothes that you don't need any more to a jumble sale or **charity shop**.
- He photographed the women to raise money for **cancer/children's/animal charities**.
- This donation is understood to be the last **charitable act** by the trust, which is soon to be dismantled.

3 Listen to the recording again. Stop the recording as necessary to complete the sentences.

1 And that made me .... and I thought …

2 So I .... from my job.

3 […] and then I got bored. And I thought, 'I'm going ....'.

4 I would say to people who are not sure about what to do with their career, that .... it.

5 But we also give .... to people who need money …

6 […] I used to be on the phone talking to .... and taking .... …

7 […] we paid for the children .... with him.

8 We've got a ...., people can phone us …

9 […] I remember another call that .... me …

10 […] I want to make a donation today because I .... and I just want to say thank you.

Some major international and UK charities:

International Federation of Red Cross and Red Crescent Societies – Worldwide humanitarian organization providing assistance without discrimination as to nationality, race, religious beliefs, class or political opinions – www.ifrc.org

UNICEF – The United Nations Children's Fund works for children's rights, their survival, development and protection – www.unicef.org

Macmillan Cancer Support (as described by Inés) – www.macmillan.org.uk

PDSA – the UK's leading veterinary/animal charity – www.pdsa.org.uk

Shelter – Shelter and homelessness charity – www.shelter.org.uk

Alzheimer's Society – care and research charity for people with Alzheimer's disease and other dementias – www.alzheimers.org.uk

The Stroke Association – supports stroke survivors, families and carers and funds research into the prevention and treatment of strokes – www.stroke.org.uk

(4) Which phrases does Inés use which have the same meanings as:

1 have a clearer view of things ....

2 be lucky ....

3 be angry ....

4 visit people ....

5 be made better ....

6 be affected by ....

7 receive money ....

8 receive news that a dangerous situation has ended ....

B ## A debate about giving to charity

(1) The two speakers discuss their preferences for different charities. Denis is from the north west of England and Sally is originally from Surrey, a county in the south east. Listen to the recording. How do the views of the speakers compare with your views on giving to charity?

(2) Which words and phrases used by the speakers have similar meanings to the following?

1 to be affected by ....

2 a very large number ....

3 good results ....

4 the right charity ....

5 advertizing ....

6 to make a deal / sign a contract ....

7 hard luck stories ....

8 meaningful ....

Useful vocabulary and phrases: charities

glamorous charities

'sexy' charities (slang for 'attractive')

publicity

charities bombard you…

A limited income

worthwhile charities

Sob stories

charitable giving

'Chuggers' is a playful, slightly derogatory term for the people Denis and Sally talk about who stop you in the street and ask you to pay a regular amount of money to a particular charity often in a slightly aggressive manner. It comes from charity + muggers = chuggers!

3 Play the recording again. Check your detailed comprehension of what the speakers say by indicating whether the statements are true or false.

	True	False
1 Denis's father received treatment for his cancer because money is given to cancer research.	....	....
2 Sally recommends giving money to large charities.	....	....
3 Sally believes that many people are keen to give money to stroke charities.	....	....
4 Denis supports animal charities.	....	....
5 Sally often gives money in supermarkets.	....	....
6 Denis offered a cigarette to a homeless man he met in Bristol. (a city in the south west of England)	....	....

4 Denis is forceful in his views and opinions and Sally is fully engaged in getting opinions from him. Listen to the recording again. Indicate whether the statements or questions are spoken by Denis [D] or Sally [S].

  1 My favourite charities are probably ones that are health-related.   [D]
  2 Has that come out of a personal experience then?   [ ]
  3 I'm inclined to now think …   [ ]
  4 I'd rather give money to smaller charities …   [ ]
  5 It would be a lot more equal, wouldn't it?   [ ]
  6 I sometimes feel a bit bad that I walk past things in supermarkets.   [ ]
  7 But don't you feel bad when …?   [ ]
  8 What I don't like is charities who bombard you …   [ ]
  9 I really hate the ones that try to sign you up for …   [ ]
10 If you've only got, say, a limited income that you can give to charity every year.   [ ]
11 Yeah, for the rest of your life.   [ ]

5 Read the questions below and then play the recording once more. Focus on listening for specific information.

  1 Why does Denis believe in prioritzing 'human' charities?
  2 What is Denis's attitude towards charities that are aggressive in the way they ask him for money?
  3 How does Sally respond to 'chuggers'?

Next steps

What would be your response to the questions above? If you are interested in finding out more about the charities mentioned in this unit, go to the respective websites. In many cases, a search for specific charities will lead you to audio and video clips of people discussing their charitable giving and to representatives of charities describing the work of their charities.

14 COLLECTING

In this unit

1 An antiques dealer from London discusses his passion for collecting.
2 A French speaker describes some unusual collections.
3 An American talks about his fascination with fountain pens.

41

A   An antiques dealer

1   Barry discusses his passion for collecting. Listen to the recording. Compare what Barry says with any expectations you might have about collecting antiques and other collectables.

Do you share Barry's passion for collecting?

Where would you look for collectable items – in specialist shops, online?

> Barry uses some particularly 'British' references such as:
> *auction houses* = auction rooms, places where public auctions take place
> *the high street* = a term generally referring to where people do their everyday shopping
> *car-boot sales* = open-air markets where goods are sold from car boots and tables set up alongside cars
> *tea caddies* = containers for storing tea

2   Listen to the recording again. Underline the items and objects which Barry mentions.

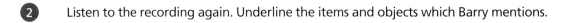

silver	gold	tea caddies	coffee-makers
paintings	sculptures	works of art	collectables
auctions	stores	car-boot sale	antique centres
furniture	cabinets	nice objects	treasures

COBUILD CHECK: collect and collection

- The jewellery is incredibly glamorous and very **collectible**.
- Today, sets of the *South Polar Times* are **rare collector's items**.
- He was a knowledgeable and enthusiastic **collector of** both china and silver.
- Jaime **made a** remarkable **collection of** 17th-century chinoiserie silver.
- Over the years, Harold **amassed** a considerable **collection of** paintings.

3 Check your understanding of the words and phrases which Barry uses by completing the gaps.

1 […] you've got to have .... it.

2 […] you can .... certain areas …

3 […] you can tour round the auctions, which I find ...., really …

4 But the important thing is, I think, is .... about it …

5 […] is to be, is to be .... whatever you want to collect …

6 […] and always .... the very best.

4 Complete the grid based on the nouns and/or adjectives used in the recording.

Noun	Adjective
passion	
collection	
antique	
	exuberant
treasure	
	enthusiastic
preoccupation	
	fanatical

B   A lifelong collector

1 Raphaël, who is originally from Nevers in France, has some interesting collections. Listen to the recording and list the items which he collects. Does his enthusiasm make you want to follow his example?

'Châteaux de Loire' – French manor houses situated in the beautiful Loire Valley area of France

Adidas, Nike, Reebok, Stan Smith, Converse – brands of trainers

Science Museum – the Science Museum located in South Kensington, London

Republic of Cameroon – country in west central Africa (capital city: Yaoundé)

2 Listen again and tick the statement which best represents what Raphaël says.

1 a His collecting habits have stayed with him all his life.   ☐

   b He tends to start collections and then move on.   ☐

2 a He has been obsessed with castles, films and stamps.   ☐

   b He has not involved his family in his collecting habits.   ☐

3 a Collecting trainers has been a constant obsession.   ☐

   b His passion for collecting trainers has come and gone.   ☐

4 a His parents share his enthusiasm for collecting trainers.   ☐

   b His parents want him to throw his old trainers away.   ☐

5 a His girlfriend never stops complaining about his obsession with trainers. ☐

  b His girlfriend complains about his shoe collection from time to time. ☐

6 a He has been to Cameroon to collect phones for a museum collection. ☐

  b He has been to Cameroon to collect phones for his own collection. ☐

COBUILD CHECK: obsession

- My son, like many of his generation, is **obsessed by** money – by how much things cost and how rich people are.
- Just over half of the 1500 young women surveyed admitted to **obsessing about** their weight.
- I could see that he was so **obsessive** about his work that he just had to succeed.
- He used to **have an obsession with** a young woman he was at high school with.
- Repeatedly washing your hands or checking if the door is locked can be telltale signs of **obsessive compulsive disorder** (OCD).

3 Raphaël speaks with a mixture of standard and colloquial English. Indicate which of the underlined words and phrases are standard [S] and which are colloquial / informal [C].

1 But what's <u>quite weird</u> with me is …   C

2 […] to be <u>obsessed</u> with Renaissance architecture ☐

3 […] to <u>compile</u> them in books ☐

4 […] <u>elaborate</u> albums ☐

5 […] <u>pretty much</u> like any teenagers ☐

6 I also <u>at some point</u> collected ☐

7 […] they <u>implore</u> me to throw them away ☐

8 […] <u>loads</u> of Japanese mobile phones ☐

9 […] exchanging <u>stuff</u> ☐

10 I'm a <u>bit of a collecting freak</u>. ☐

C   A fountain pen enthusiast

1 Listen to the recording. Does David engage you with his enthusiasm for his collection? Does he make you want to start collecting fountain pens? Why or why not?

2 Can you answer the comprehension questions below after you have listened to the recording or do you need to listen again?

1 How old was David when he bought his first fountain pen?

2 Why did David buy his first fountain pen?

3 How many pens did David have when he started to refer to having a 'collection'?

4   When were fountain pens made which are now classed as 'vintage'?

5   How many pens does David currently own?

6   What is his most prized pen?

Clear usage: developing a narrative

Note how David talks about how he became interested in collecting pens. He uses a range of past tenses to narrate his story.

'I *got started* collecting.' (informal alternative to *I started*)

'I *started off* relatively simply.'

'I *didn't intend* it to be a collection.'

'My handwriting was good because *I'd (I had) invested in* these pens.'

'I *was paying* more attention to my writing.'

---

3 Now listen to the recording again to check that you understand the exact words that David uses. The gaps mainly represent language which shows how much David is attached to his collection.

1   I started off relatively simply with a .... fountain pen.

2   […] one purchase .... another …

3   […] I started to develop fountain-pen ....

4   I would see other people with .... fountain pens …

5   […] I saw a beautiful pen there and I just really, really .... by that pen …

6   At about that time my handwriting was really good because .... these pens …

7   […] I also .... attention to my writing.

8   […] my .... is a Japanese pen.

4 Listen again. Which phrases does David use which have similar meanings to the following?

1   I always had very bad handwriting. ....

2   a fairly cheap fountain pen. ....

3   I began to feel jealous of other people's fountain pens. ....

4   I'd spent money on these pens. ....

5   There's an American make called Parker. ....

6   I don't show them in a glass cabinet. ....

7   My most treasured possession. ....

8   It has very beautiful details on it. ....

Next steps

If you would like to hear more from Barry or from David talking about his other passion (collecting ukuleles), go to **www.collinselt.com/englishforlife/extras**. Go online to find video and audio recordings of people talking about collectables which you are interested in.

15 MUSIC

In this unit

1 Two Chinese speakers discuss their views on traditional and current Chinese music.

2 Two Indian speakers talk about the Bollywood genre of music and films.

A Chinese music

44

1 Zhang is from Suzhou in Jiangsu province; Wang is from Huaibei in Anhui province. Listen to the recording. Who do you think is older, Wang (who speaks first) or Zhang? Does age or generation influence the type of music you listen to?

2 Listen to the recording again to check your detailed comprehension of the dialogue. Are these statements true or false according to what the speakers say? If you are familiar with the music being discussed, of course, you may or may not agree with the opinions expressed.

		True	False
1	Wang prefers Chinese classical music.	....	....
2	Zhang last listened to Chun Jiang Hua Yue Ye ten years ago.	....	....
3	Zhang thinks that rock music is very popular in China.	....	....
4	Tang Dynasty are currently a popular Chinese band.	....	....
5	Wang says that she is too young to have listened to Tang Dynasty.	....	....
6	Rock music is popular in China.	....	....

COBUILD CHECK: music genres

• The music ranges from **rock** to classical.
• Gallagher had displayed little interest in rock music, preferring to listen to **hip hop**.
• She liked clothes, dancing, **pop** music, and sports.
• The ensemble plays a wide range of **classical** music including the works of Mozart and Beethoven.
• He introduced **mainstream** country music to a lot of music fans.
• The **indie** rock legends headlined the bash alongside Radiohead.
• Camden is one of the focus points for **alternative** music in London, and is famous for its live music venues.

Listening tip: accents and non-standard English

Zhang and Wang are fluent speakers of English, but you may not be familiar with their accents or the non-standard forms of English which they use. Play the recording several times and refer to the transcript to familiarize yourself with the way they speak. Note some 'standard' English alternatives to the language they use. Did these 'language mistakes' cause you any listening problems?

Wang: I don't know how to translate.
Standard: *I don't know how to translate **it**.*

Wang: I haven't listened to that since, like, ten years ago.
Standard: *I haven't listened to that for about ten years.*

Zhang: That band was dismissed, like, five years ago.
Standard: *That band broke up about five years ago.*

Zhang: It's a huge popular at that time.
Standard: *It was hugely popular at that time.*

Wang: I think I'm too young at the time so I never heard this rock band before.
Standard: *I think I was too young at the time so I have never heard this rock band before.*

3 Can you remember the words used by the speakers? Try to do the exercise without listening back. Then, listen to check if you were right. The first letter of the missing word is provided to give you a clue.

1 I like to listen to them sometimes when I'm a ....

2 They will I .... forever.

3 They have traditional Chinese e .... in their performance.

4 They (Tang Dynasty) used to have a very p .... song.

5 I've never heard this rock b .... before.

6 Rock's never been m .... in China.

4 Zhang refers to the music of 'Tang Dynasty' as being 'a huge popular' at the time (rather than the standard English 'hugely popular'). Many speakers do not use adjectives (huge) and adverbs (hugely) as prescribed in standard English. For practice, complete the following table

Verb	Adjective	Adverb
– *(no verb)*	huge	hugely
to perfect		
to strengthen		
to sooth		
– *(no verb)*	particular	
to prefer		
to notice	strong	

Clear usage: use of 'since' + 'ago'

Note that Zhang says:

'I haven't listened to that since, like, ten years ago.'

This is not standard English but many speakers of English do use 'since' with 'ago'.

Standard uses:
I haven't listened to that since I was ten years old.
I haven't listened to that for ten years.
The last time I listened to it was ten years ago.

B   Indian music and Bollywood

1 Listen to the recording. What do you already know about Bollywood films and music? Does anything Krishna and Neeraj say surprise you?

> 'Bollywood' refers to the film industry which is based in Mumbai (Bombay), in the state of Maharashtra in the west of India. The music and dance routines are key features of Bollywood films and, as Krishna says, many of the songs become 'big hits'.

2 Now listen to the recording again. Tick the statements which best represent what the speakers say about Bollywood and the audience for the films and music.

1 Many Indians dream of being involved in Bollywood films. ☐
2 Bollywood has always tried to be very different from Hollywood. ☐
3 Some Bollywood actors are actually worshipped. ☐
4 There are more songs and dances in Bollywood films than in Hollywood films. ☐
5 Young people tend to watch Bollywood films only at the weekends. ☐
6 Bollywood is mainly aimed at the older age group. ☐
7 A lot of songs are performed while the actors run around trees. ☐
8 There is a global audience for Bollywood. ☐

Clear usage: use of 'get' instead of 'be' in passive sentences

Krishna says that many people want to *get hauled into* movies. In this context, *get* is used informally instead of the more formal 'be'.

They want to **get seen** (be seen) at movie premieres.

They want to **get driven** (be driven) to festivals.

He'd like to **get introduced** (be introduced) to some music producers.

Did you **get invited** (Were you invited) to the party after the concert?

> Note that 'hauled' is an unusual word to use in this context. Many people would like to 'get involved' in Bollywood, whereas to be 'hauled in' in standard usage implies being made to do something (against your will).

3 Focus on some key information provided by the speakers by completing the gaps in these sentences. Listen to the recording and pause it as necessary.

1 [...] it's a big .... for a lot of Indians.
2 [...] it has actually .... the years, ...
3 [...] we are trying to .... from what happens ...
4 [...] compared to Hollywood, ... that stuff ...
5 [...] they also have a good amount of ....
6 [...] Bollywood movies are .... over the world simultaneously,..

COBUILD CHECK: the music industry

- The Beatles' song 'Yesterday' was played more than six million times on US radio, and more than 2,200 other artists went on to **record** the **song**.
- During six years with Jive records, she **released** five **albums**, including 'The Best Of'.
- The band will **perform** live in the city's Convention Hall.
- Formats such as MP3 have made it easy to **download music** from the Internet, legally or illegally.
- The Irish **music festival**, now in its fourth year, will have three stages and feature several new bands.
- Every track ever recorded can be instantly available to music **fans**.
- Glasgow was bidding to host the MTV music **awards ceremony**.

4 Which words and expressions used by Krishna and Neeraj have similar meanings to the words in brackets?

1 Bollywood is (commemorating) .... one hundred years of cinema in India.
2 It has (grown/developed) .... over the years.
3 We've started (dealing with) .... the issues of today.
4 We are trying to (reproduce/copy) .... what happens in Hollywood.
5 They are (mad about) .... some of the songs.
6 It's a big (leisure activity) .... for them.
7 There is a lot of (growth/development) .... that has happened around music also in India.
8 The films are released all over the world (at the same time) ....

Next steps

If you have not listened to Chinese or Indian music, are you encouraged to do so from what you have heard in these recordings? Go online to find examples of the music mentioned and compare your opinions with those of the speakers. Zhang and Wang's recording continues on **www.collinselt.com/englishforlife/extras.**

16 ENVIRONMENT

In this unit

1 Nick, a Londoner who works for the Zoological Society of London (ZSL), discusses the 'Net-Works' project in the Philippines.

2 A Korean English teacher discusses the importance of everyday recycling.

46

A An environmental project in the Philippines

1 The 'Net-Works' project involves converting old fishing nets into another useable product. Read the questions below. Then listen to the recording and compare your answers with what Nick says.

1 Which product do you think this might be?

2 How long can plastic last before it degrades?

3 What do you think 'ghost-fishing' might be?

Clear usage: passive and active simple-present forms

Note how Nick mainly uses passive verb forms as he describes the situation in the Philippines. The passive is commonly used when describing a process. If Nick had wanted to focus on those responsible for the process he would more likely have used the active form – as he did in the final example below.

He says: 'Discarded fishing nets are made from nylon …'

He could have said: *They make (discarded) fishing nets from nylon.*

He says: 'It is used in fishing nets.'

He could have said: *They use it in fishing nets.*

He says: 'It's called "ghost-fishing".'

He could have said: *They call it 'ghost-fishing'.*

But he also says: 'They don't throw them into the sea.'

He could have said: *They are not thrown into the sea.*

Useful vocabulary and phrases: Net-Works

a conservation charity	a really exciting initiative
discarded fishing nets	monofilament fishing nets
waste-management services	to ensnare marine life
ghost-fishing	the crabs die and rot
seaweed farming	commercial-scale fisheries
community-based supply chains	community groups aggregate the nets

2 Check that you understand the following words and phrases which Nick uses. Then listen to the recording again and answer the questions.

1 What does the 'Net-Works' project do?

2 What uses of nylon are mentioned?

3 At what point do fishermen throw their nets away?

4 Where do the fishermen currently tend to dump (throw away) their nets?

5 What is the problem caused by 'ghost-fishing'?

6 What do the community groups do with the nets before they are sold?

COBUILD CHECK: protecting the environment

- Today, world marine life is under threat from **pollution**.
- They want an ecologically **sustainable** forest industry that is not dominated by the negative impacts of land-clearing and wildlife destruction.
- The university announced its plan to switch to electricity generated from **renewable resources**.
- The burning of the rainforest is thought to be contributing to **global warming**.
- **Carbon dioxide emissions**, mainly from burning fossil fuels, are thought to be a principle cause of global warming.
- Your **carbon footprint** is a measure of the carbon dioxide released into the atmosphere by your activities in a given time.

3 Listen again. Check your understanding by completing the gaps.

1 Um, Net-Works is a .... um ... very different ...

2 [...] and after two or three months these nets .... and they don't catch fish as well as they used to.

3 The plastic can .... before it degrades.

4 Now, many of these places are ...., so any additional pressure...

5 The fishers in the Central Philippines that we work with .... on the sea.

6 [...] we have set up .... to be able to collect nets off the beaches ...

7 [...] and then the community- .... all of those nets, ...

8 [...] Slovenia, where there's the .... in the world ... um ... for nylon.

4 Complete the phrases by matching the two sentence halves.

1 We run a project ...   a get damaged and ripped.

2 The objective of Net-Works is to ...   b turn old nets into carpet tiles.

3 The nets get ...   c ensnare marine life.

4 At this point the fishermen often ...   d degrades.

5 After two or three months these nets ...   e rot.

6 The plastic can last for up to six hundred years before it ... f throw the nets away.

7 The fish die, the crabs die and they ...   g called Net-Works.

8 It (the plastic) can continue to catch and ...   h damaged after a bit of time.

B ## Recycling in South Korea

Listen to Jooyoung as she talks about the importance of recycling. If you have not listened to Korean speakers of English before, you may need to listen to the recording a few times to get used to Jooyoung's accent. Focus on understanding her main message and make notes about three things.

General household recycling

....

Recycling of food waste

....

Efforts to reduce CO_2 emissions

....

COBUILD CHECK: recycling and waste

- All of the packaging is made from **recyclable materials**.
- Recyclable materials are taken away, sorted and sent to the appropriate **recycling plant**.
- In California, a target was set to reduce waste **going to landfill** by 50%.
- Under the scheme, those who **sort household waste** into categories such as paper and glass would pay nothing.
- Companies have adopted **waste disposal** methods which reduce pollution levels.
- Household waste is processed and prepared for recycling, **incineration**, or landfill.

2 Read through the words and phrases below. Then listen to the recording and identify them as Jooyoung speaks. She pronounces some of the words below in a way which may not be familiar to you but others will be clear and easy to follow.

they have more and more effort	dead batteries and plastics
keep the environment clean	Usually Korean food has a lot of liquid
system of recycling	I think this method
divide their waste by category	everyday household effort

3 Listen to the recording again and answer the questions to check your detailed comprehension of what Jooyoung says.

1 How many recycling containers are located in her apartment block collection point?

....

2 What are the container name tags which Jooyoung mentions?

....

3 What might happen to people if they do not put their waste in the correct container?

....

4 Why is everyone in Korea trying to reduce the amount of food waste?

....

5 What type of assignment are elementary school children given every summer?

....

6 Why are the children given this assignment?

....

7 What is the potential impact of this assignment?

....

Clear usage: consequences of action and inaction

Jooyoung says:

'If we keep making this kind of effort, maybe the environment can get better.'

In other words there is a good chance of a positive outcome if action is taken. We can also use 'providing', 'provided', and 'as long as' to predict a positive outcome.
Providing we continue to make every effort, we will make the environment better.
Provided we keep recycling, we will reduce the amount of waste which goes to landfill.
As/So long as we do this, things will improve.

Jooyoung uses 'otherwise' to predict a negative outcome if something is not done – in this case she discusses what might happen if she does not put her recycling into the correct container!

'Otherwise the handyman comes along and gives you a warning.'

Other standard English examples using 'otherwise':
Make sure you don't put out your rubbish until 7 o'clock in the morning; otherwise you'll be fined.
You need to separate your waste; otherwise the refuse collectors will not take it.

---

4 Listen to the recording again. Number the phrases which Jooyoung uses in the order you hear them. Play them again until they become more familiar.

1 […] the most commonplace environmental effort … `1`

2 […] the machine actually weighs the food waste … ☐

3 I think we can actually reduce the amount of CO_2 we produce. ☐

4 […] sometimes you can be fined … ☐

5 […] five different categories … ☐

6 […] a big collection point … ☐

7 So there is a school assignment about CO_2 reduction … ☐

8 […] everyday household effort … ☐

Next steps

Are you interested in helping with exciting environmental projects such as the one described here? Are you in tune with Jooyoung's enthusiasm for recycling? If you would like to hear more from Nick about the uses made of recycled nylon by Aquafil, go to **www.collinselt.com/englishforlife/extras**
Check the ZSL website (www.zsl.org) where you can find a page dedicated to the Net-Works project.
Go online to find out more about recycling programmes in Korea and in other countries.

17 WEDDINGS

In this unit

1 Two Indian friends describe Indian weddings.

2 Nikki from Scotland talks about some differences between Scottish and American weddings.

A Indian weddings

48

Krishna and Neeraj, who are from Bangalore and New Delhi in India respectively, focus on the cultural aspects of an Indian wedding. Listen to the recording. Do Krishna and Neeraj confirm what you already knew about Indian weddings? Are you surprised by anything they say? Do not worry about understanding every word, but try to understand the main points which they make.

COBUILD CHECK: spending money

- The **cost** of the average British wedding has exceeded £10,000.
- They could not **afford** a holiday that year.
- A household's major weekly **expenditure** is on food.
- They were planning a **lavish** wedding on the Caribbean island of Anguilla.
- Examples of **extravagant** spending include an £88,000 reception desk.
- The fact we'd spent so much on creating a slick office might seem **wasteful**.
- It's your fault because you were too **mean** to pay a roofer to clear the gutter.
- The traditional tavernas offer much better **value for money**.

Listen to the recording again and answer the questions below. Again, do not worry if you cannot understand everything that is said. You can check the transcript later.

1 How long do wedding celebrations last in India? ....

2 Are most weddings 'arranged' or are they love matches? ....

3 What is a lot of money spent on before a wedding? ....

4 What differences does Krishna observe about weddings held in the south and north of India? ....
....

5 What kind of event does Neeraj mention as being arranged typically in Northern India by the groom's family? ....

6 How many people attended Krishna's wedding? ....

7 What concerns Krishna about the weddings of rich families in India? ....

....

8 Do only rich families spend more than they can actually afford?

....

Clear usage: present continuous passive

Note how these speakers often use the continuous present passive form. The continuous form is frequently used by Indian speakers of English where other English speakers might use the simple form.

'There are always some meals being organized.' *(There are always some meals organized.)*
'A lot of money is being wasted.' *(A lot of money is wasted.)*
'A lot of effort is being put in there also.' *(A lot of effort is put in.)*
'Very expensive gifts are being exchanged.' *(Very expensive gifts are exchanged.)*

---

3 Listen to the recording again and this time pay special attention to the words and phrases actually used. Pause the recording if necessary to complete the gaps.

1 [...] the majority of the weddings .... in India.

2 [...] usually it's never ...., like how Krishna said, it can go on for several days.

3 [...] there's always .... – a lot of music and dance.

4 So it was ...., with so many people attending the ceremony.

5 [...] we .... for such a big crowd.

6 [...] the people who come and attend the wedding, they .... and also gift ...

7 [...] sometimes they do .... money, ...

8 [...] you end up spending more money than .... to do on a wedding in India!

B ## Preparing for a Scottish – American wedding

49

Nikki is soon to get married. She talks to her friend Lorna (who is also from Scotland) about some differences between Scottish and American weddings.

What questions would you want to ask Nikki about her wedding plans? Compare what she is planning with any weddings which you have been to.

Nikki mentions these particularly Scottish items:
a kilt – a type of skirt traditionally worn by Scottish men.
tartan – a design for cloth traditionally associated with Scotland
But not these...
a ceilidh – Scottish weddings often are followed by a ceilidh, with traditional Gaelic and Scottish folk music and dancing
bagpipes – probably the best-known Scottish musical instrument
the saltire – the name of the national flag of Scotland
a quaich (described by Nikki in the extended online recording – go to
www.collinselt.com/englishforlife/extras to hear the description)

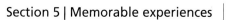

2 Play the recording again and answer the questions to test your comprehension.

1 How are the wedding plans going? ....
2 When is the wedding taking place? ....
3 What does a 'rehearsal dinner' involve? ....
4 When does a 'rehearsal dinner' take place? ....
5 How does Nikki feel about having a 'rehearsal dinner'? ....
6 Which American tradition is Nikki really nervous about? ....
7 Who will be wearing kilts at the wedding? ....
8 Will the kilt worn be in the 'family tartan'? ....
9 Why do the non-Scottish guests want to wear kilts? ....
10 How successful does Lorna predict that the wedding will be? ....

Useful vocabulary and phrases: weddings

bride and groom

best man and the maid of honour

wedding ceremony

usher (groomsman – [US])

stag party (bachelor party – [US]), hen party (bachelorette party – [US])

wedding reception

guest list

bride-to-be

my mother-in-law-to-be (my future mother-in-law)

---

3 Complete these sentences with words and phrases from the box above. In some cases, there is more than one possible answer

1 Have you ever been to .... in a castle? I went to one last week.
2 John chose his best friend from school to be .... at his wedding.
3 John and his friends went to Vilnius in Lithuania for his ....
4 It was very difficult to limit .... for the wedding.
5 .... met when they were both on holiday in Paris.
6 My .... is nothing like my mum, but they get on very well all the same.
7 She found it difficult to choose just one .... She has so many friends.
8 Julia didn't want to have a wild .... She just wanted to spend a quiet evening at home with her close friends.

4 Nikki and Lorna use a lot of colloquial and idiomatic language. Check that you understand the meanings of the phrases below. Then listen to the recording again and write down some standard equivalent phrases.

1 A little bit scary   ....rather frightening.........
2 It's just weird, like ...   .

3 Stuff that I expected …   ....

4 A massive thing in America …   ....

5 a kind of run-through   ....

5   Lorna listens attentively to what Nikki says about her wedding plans. She responds with empathetic statements and asks follow-up questions. Focus on what Lorna says as you listen again and complete the gaps.

1   Oh, you .... so excited.

2   I've never ....

3   What does that ...., a rehearsal dinner?

4   I suppose it .... I'm sure you're both really excited..

5   So you can .... that way, I suppose.

6   And you've not told me .... part: is Patrick going to wear a kilt?

7   What .... ? … is your dad going to wear a kilt …?

8   So it sounds like ....

Clear usage: describing future events

This recording focuses on Nikki's plans for her wedding. Note the different ways she refers to this future event.

'Present continuous' used to refer to the future where the arrangement already exists:
'We're having the wedding in Scotland.'
'What about the rehearsal dinner – When is that happening?'
'We're not having one of those.'
'I know nobody's using our tartan'

'Going to' also used to refer to future plans:
'We're going to have it engraved.'
'We're going to do a 'quaich' ceremony.'
'He is going to wear a kilt.'

'Will' to refer to what will happen at the wedding:
'Will it be your tartan?'
'All the wedding party will be (in kilts).'
'My dad'll be in a kilt.'

'Will' is mainly used when referring to more impersonal information about future arrangements.

Next steps

You can hear more from Nikki and Lorna on **www.collinselt.com/englishforlife/extras.** There are other recordings of Krishna and Neeraj in this book if you would like further practice in understanding Indian speakers of English.

18 RISING TO A CHALLENGE

In this unit

1 An American tourist describes some difficult situations she encountered in the Seychelles.

2 A British volunteer at the Glastonbury music festival describes her experience.

A   Adventures while travelling

50

1 Melissa, who is originally from Connecticut in the north east of the USA, has returned from a holiday in the Seychelles. Listen to the recording. What were the two situations described by Melissa which she found so frightening?

2 Check the vocabulary below in a dictionary or **www.collinsdictionary.com/cobuild** and then listen to the recording again. Now answer the questions to check your detailed comprehension of Melissa's story.

crabs	to scramble
the jungle canopy	crab claws
spiders	tortoises
bugs	to scurry

1 What was special about Melissa's trip to the Seychelles?
2 Why was the walk through the jungle so frightening?
3 Why did Melissa and her husband go out to dinner in local restaurants?
4 Why are 'coconut crabs' called 'coconut crabs'?
5 What did the crabs do when Melissa started screaming?

COBUILD CHECK: hilarious or terrifying?

- An image on a TV screen can be made frightening or **hilarious** by the music soundtrack.
- She could clear a dance floor with her **hysterical** `River Dance' impersonation.
- It may seem **comic** now, but it was not quite so comic when you claimed that you had a gun.
- She has no idea why she finds flying so **terrifying**.
- Herbert nearly lost his foot in a **horrific** accident.
- The drug can help relieve the **distressing** symptoms of anxiety.
- He has become crippled by fear as a result of one **alarming** experience.

Clear usage: wish

When referring to the fact that there were large spiders in the forest, Melissa says:
'We wish *we knew* that from the beginning.'

This statement is clear in its meaning but is not standard usage.
Note the standard English form after wish used to express regrets about the past:
We wish **we had known** that from the beginning.
I wish **you had told** me earlier.

wish followed by a past form of the verb (as used by Melissa) is normally used to express regret or a desire for something which is not possible now or in the future:
I wish **I could afford** to go to the Seychelles on holiday.
I wish **I knew** the answer.

3 Melissa uses some colourful colloquial phrases. Match the phrases she uses with a similar phrase below.

1	a total blast	**a**	totally dark
2	a last hurrah	**b**	absolutely everywhere
3	a close call	**c**	very relaxed
4	take your life into your hands	**d**	risk everything
5	pitch black	**e**	understand something after a bad experience
6	literally every inch	**f**	a near escape
7	learn a lesson	**g**	a final good experience
8	laid back	**h**	great fun

Clear usage: avoiding reported speech

Melissa tells a dramatic story and does not use standard 'reported speech' forms as she wants to retain the drama of her conversations.
Note also her use of *'like'* and *'sort of'* and even *'sort of like'*:

'So it was *sort of like*, "this is the trail, this is where you go …".'
'Um, nothing *like*, "watch out for the animals".'
'We *sort of* said to the guides, "those spiders, by any chance were we taking our lives into our own hands?".'
'And they said, "Oh no, totally harmless".'

Compare with the same statements put into standard reported-speech forms:

So they told us where the trail was and where to go.
They didn't tell us to watch out for the animals.
We asked the guides if the spiders were dangerous.
They told us that they were totally harmless.

4 Listen once more and complete the phrases relating to Melissa's challenging experience.

1 [...] were these spiders .... that were, you know, within three or four feet ...

2 [...] the entire canopy of the jungle .... with these spiders.

3 My husband is very tall so he .... constantly out of fear.

4 [...] as soon as the sun set, these crabs .... the beach.

5 [...] they can open coconuts with ....

6 [...] they would .... back into the jungle...

7 [...] there was about 5 minutes to 10 minutes of .... on my part.

8 [...] my husband thought it was ....

B   A difficult job

51

1 Lucy is from the south of England. She talks about her experience of working at the Glastonbury music festival in Somerset in the south west of England.

Listen to the recording. Glastonbury is one of the largest music festivals in the UK and is held in June. English weather is famously unpredictable! Compare what you might expect to happen at such a festival with Lucy's experience of being there.

Listening tip: pronunciation

Note when Lucy drops 't's and pronounces 'l's as if they are 'w's at the end of words. This is common pronunciation for many UK speakers, particularly in the south of England. As you listen, focus on the words highlighted in the following expressions and note Lucy's pronunciation. Compare this with how she pronounces 't's and 'l's in other words.

2 From your memory of playing the recording once, circle the words which describe Lucy's experience at Glastonbury. Then listen again and check your answers.

1 This was Lucy's *first / second* experience of Glastonbury.

2 The festival site was *very muddy / clean and tidy* when we arrived.

3 People were *very depressed by / unaffected by* the bad weather.

4 She slept *well / badly* in her tent.

5 She *had to / wanted to* stay on after the festival ended.

6 She was *happy / sad* that the festival was over.

7 If she goes back to Glastonbury, she will arrange *similar / more comfortable* accommodation.

Glastonbury festival is held every year or every two years at Pilton farm in Somerset. It was started by a local farmer, Michael Eavis, as long ago as 1970 as a small event and has grown to become one of the largest music festivals in the world, attended by around 175,000 people each year. Many major bands and singers have performed at the festival (www.glastonburyfestivals.co.uk)

3 Lucy uses a lot of colloquial, informal language. Listen out for the colloquial phrases which she uses which have similar meanings to the standard phrases below.

Standard	Colloquial/informal
1 People who attend a festival.	....
2 The weather was reasonable.	....
3 it became very difficult	....
4 unusual/unexpected things	....
5 to meet by chance	....
6 it was raining hard.	....
7 keep going	....
8 to go 'up-market' camping	....

4 Listen to the recording again. Try to work out the meanings of these words and phrases from the context of the recording and then check if you understood correctly by referring to a dictionary or **www.collinsdictionary.com/cobuild.**

1 a house that was supposed to be **flood-resistant …**

2 the fields were all **pristine …**

3 the rain was **tipping down …**

4 **trudge** through the mud …

5 Massive crowds all **congregate** around the main stage.

6 we had to **dismantle** the structure …

7 it was really **arduous** …

8 because I was **scarred by** the mud.

9 the window of opportunity.

10 I'm a bit of **a stickler for** home comforts.

Making the most of opportunities

Lucy talks about going back to Glastonbury but says that the 'window of opportunity hasn't opened'.

Note these other phrases:

She seized the opportunity to work at the festival.

She saw it as a great opportunity.

She didn't want to miss the opportunity.

She took full advantage of the opportunity.

Next steps

Would you rather trudge through a jungle or trudge through the mud at a music festival? Are you more inspired to follow in Melissa's or Lucy's footsteps? Go online to find out more about the spiders and crabs in the Seychelles (as well as the beautiful beaches!)

Go online to find videos of Glastonbury festival: music and interviews with musicians and festival-goers.

19 HOLIDAY DESTINATIONS

In this unit

1 Two British friends talk about their experiences of travelling in Australia.

2 Saya from Japan recommends the best time to visit her country and talks about the Obon festival.

A   A trip to Australia

52

1 Laura and Jude talk about their travels to Australia. Laura is originally from Birmingham, the second largest city in England. Jude is from the north west of the country.

Listen to the recording. In your opinion, which are the most memorable experiences described by the speakers?

2 Both speakers are very enthusiastic about the time they spent in Australia. Listen to the recording again and tick the phrases which you hear them use to express their enthusiasm.

1	It was amazing.	☐
2	We had such a ball.	☐
3	It was unbelievable.	☐
4	[…] which was really fantastic.	☐
5	[…] which was really cool.	☐
6	That must have been wonderful.	☐
7	That was really special.	☐
8	Awesome!	☐
9	It was so cute.	☐
10	Koalas are gorgeous.	☐

3 Do you know the words and phrases below? If they are new to you, can you understand them from the context of the recording and from what you might expect to hear given your knowledge of Australia? After listening, check meanings in your dictionary or at **www.collinsdictionary.com/cobuild.**

cutting edge	bouncer	cores	jetlag
coastal route	boiling	koala bear sanctuary	pouch
tame	shade	joey	

Listening tip: showing empathy with the speaker

Laura knows that Sydney, Australia, is probably very hot at Christmas, so responds to Jude's news by saying '(It) *must have been* hot'. Later she also responds when Jude tells her about her journey to see the 'Twelve Apostles' with 'That *must have been* beautiful'.

Using so-called 'modals of deduction' is an excellent way of demonstrating empathy with the speaker.

That **can't have been** a good experience.
That **must have been** very disappointing.
It **must have been** terrifying.

4 Practise the vocabulary which Laura and Jude use. Complete the gaps with words from the box.

boiling	cute	cutting edge	lovely
amazing	glamorous	tame	cosmopolitan

1 The animals were so adorable and sweet – they were really ....
2 The architecture was very modern, very ....
3 It was so hot we had to stay in the shade. It was absolutely ....
4 The koalas were so .... that we were able to hold them.
5 The holiday was .... I've never been to so many beautiful places.
6 We stayed in a very .... hotel. All the rooms were individually decorated.
7 It was a great place to stay. The people were .... and the food was fantastic.
8 People have moved to Melbourne from all over the world. It is a very .... city.

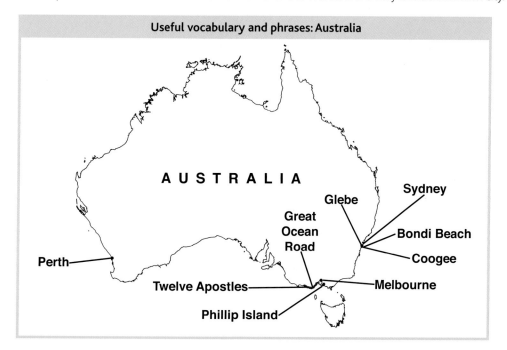

Useful vocabulary and phrases: Australia

5 From your recollection of the recording, which of the statements represent what was said? Listen to the recording again to check your answers.

1 a Jude has been to Sydney. ☐

  b Jude and Laura have been to Sydney. ☐

2 a Jude's friend was getting married. ☐

  b Jude's boyfriend's friend was getting married. ☐

3 a The weather was very hot in Sydney at Christmas time. ☐

  b The weather was very cold in Sydney at Christmas time. ☐

4 a Jude got sunburnt. ☐

  b Jude did not get sunburnt. ☐

5 a The kangaroos she saw wanted to avoid the sun. ☐

  b The kangaroos she saw wanted to stay in the sun. ☐

6 a Only Jude has seen the 'Twelve Apostles' at sunset. ☐

  b Both Laura and Jude have seen the 'Twelve Apostles' at sunset. ☐

B A trip to Japan

1 Saya is from Fukuoka in the south of Japan. Listen to the recording. Focus on the key points she makes without worrying about understanding every word. Summarize briefly what she says about:

1 the weather in Japan in August

2 the Obon festival

Clear usage: making recommendations

Saya recommends the best time to visit Japan by saying that it 'will be a good time to go' during the Obon festival. This is a clear message simply expressed. Some other useful phrases for making recommendations:

I wouldn't recommend going in August – it is very hot then.
The best time to go would be during the Obon festival.
Why not go during the winter?
I think you ought to go during the summer months.
My recommendation would be to go in June.

2 Play the recording again and answer the questions to check your comprehension.

1 Despite the weather, why might August be a good month to visit Japan?

....

2 If you are a tourist, what problem might you have during the Obon festival?

....

3 Is Obon celebrated more in Tokyo or in rural areas?

....

4 Do Saya's parents live in Tokyo?

....

5 What happens on 13th August?

....

6 What happens on 15th August?

....

7 What is a 'yukata'?

....

COBUILD CHECK: describing the weather

- It was **cooler** than the day before.
- The weather was still grey and **overcast**.
- It was a **boiling hot** day but the windows were shut.
- August is usually hot and **muggy**, with 95% humidity.
- The boat ran aground in **stormy** weather off the Finnish coast.

 Compare some of the non-standard English used by Saya with standard English:

Non-standard	Standard
on August	in August
you are very sweating and sticky	you get very sweaty and sticky
I not recommend you go	I don't recommend you to go
especially if you are go	especially if you go
I'm from really rural area	I'm from a really rural area
so most of the shop and supermarket will be close	so most of the shops and supermarkets will be closed
it's meant to be happen everywhere	it's meant to happen everywhere

Now rewrite these other examples of her non-standard usage. Do the 'non-standard' forms actually cause you any comprehension problems? Note that Saya might use non-standard forms, but her level of English should not be underestimated.

Non-standard	Standard
1 [...] someone who from Tokyo …	....
2 [...] if you go to rural area …	....
3 [...] then we having a traditional meal …	....
4 So it more like a religious thing to me …	....
5 [...] you can really enjoy it to wear.	....
6 So looks like kimono but much, like, lighter …	....

Next steps

If you have difficulty understanding the speakers in this unit, is this mainly because of how fast they speak, their pronunciation or the grammar (correct/complex or non-standard/simple) which they use? Reflect on how you should speak as clearly as possible to ensure that you help **your** listeners to understand **you**. There is more from Saya talking about the Obon festival and from Laura and Jude on **www.collinselt.com/englishforlife/extras**.

20 LIFE-CHANGING EVENTS

In this unit

1 Oscar describes his experience of sailing across the Atlantic.
2 Rachael talks about how she received a donor kidney.
3 Rachael expresses her gratitude to the kidney donor.

A   **A challenge at sea**

54

1 Listen to the recording. Oscar is from the south of England. Focus on understanding some key points from Oscar's account of his 20-day adventure. Make some notes about

- where he sailed from and to.
- what he enjoyed most about the experience.
- whether he would recommend others to take part in the race.

> The Canaries = the Canary Islands, off the west coast of Africa.
> St Lucia = an island country in the East Caribbean Sea
> The trade winds = winds which blow towards the equator from the tropics; they blow from the north east in the Northern Hemisphere and from the south east in the Southern Hemisphere.
> Port = the left side of a boat when facing the bow
> Starboard = the right side of a boat when facing the bow
> GPS (Global Positioning System) = satellite-based navigation system that gives information about location in all weather conditions
> Bay of Biscay = a large bay in the Atlantic near Spain and France
> The 'south coast' = the south coast of England
> Chichester = a small city near the south coast of England

2 Listen to the recording again and answer the questions.

1 What does ARC stand for?
2 What kind of wind is indicated by force twelve on the Beaufort scale?
3 What force of wind did Oscar experience throughout his journey?
4 Did he enjoy the isolation during the journey?
5 What means of communication was available to him?
6 What navigation equipment did he use during the voyage?
7 Was Oscar new to sailing prior to the voyage?
8 What is the 'vision' which will stay with Oscar forever?

Clear usage: talking about past possibilities

Oscar says: 'The satellite telephone would have been used.'

Oscar uses the past passive form of the modal verb *'would'*. He states that the satellite telephone was not used but there was a possibility that it *'would have been used'* if necessary. Note these examples of past modal forms which could be used to talk about past possibilities (passive and active):

It would have been used if the weather had turned bad.
We would have used it if the weather had turned bad.
It could have been used.
We could have used it.
It might have been used.
We might have used it.

3 Now listen to the recording again and complete the gaps to focus on the actual words and phrases which Oscar uses.

1 The sailing race .... was called the ARC, which stands for ...

2 The winds .... on a Beaufort scale which is ...

3 [...] the tea clippers etc, ... would use those winds to trade effectively around the world ...

4 Because once you've left the start line, you .... the night.

5 [...] and there's no one that's going to be able to .... or— or help you if ...

6 If there was a death on the ship, the satellite telephone .... used.

7 [...] then, looking at the horizon, you can .... where you are ...

8 And obviously you're .... on a chart all the way along.

9 I .... it before and so I was very excited by it.

10 So I was, I was .... what was going on.

Listening tip: contracted speech

Oscar says: 'The satellite telephone would have been used.'

Notice Oscar's pronunciation /would ev bin/ where he uses contracted forms.

Listen to the recording whilst reading the transcript to focus on how contracted forms are used in standard spoken English. These shortened forms are often the cause of listening-comprehension difficulties.

4 Which words and phrases used by Oscar have similar meanings to the following?

1 to participate

2 a long journey by sea

3 the scale used for measuring wind speed

4 the remoteness

5 unclear/dim lights

6 to rescue you

7 at its height/peak

8 the captain

9 to learn how things are done

10 to have an understanding of what was happening

B   A life-saving operation

1 Rachael, who is from Newcastle in the north east of England, tells a powerful and moving story of how she received a donor kidney after spending years on dialysis.

Ensure that you are familiar with these terms which Rachael uses before listening. Check the meanings in a dictionary or at **www.collinsdictionary.com/cobuild.**

blood group	steroid injections	dialysis	a transplant
kidney	a perfect match	to kick-start	

2 Now listen to the recording and answer the questions. Pause the recording as necessary.

1 Why could Rachael's parents not donate one of their kidneys?

2 Why did Rachael think it was not fair to ask her brother to donate a kidney?

3 What was she doing and what was she about to do when the call came to tell her there was a kidney for her?

4 How long was she given to get to the hospital?

5 When she got to hospital, how long did Rachael have to wait for her operation?

6 How did she feel once the kidney had 'kick-started'?

Rachael uses the expression to 'whip out' a kidney. 'Whip out' normally refers to removing something quickly and easily, so this is a rather unusual usage!

3 If you were speaking to Rachael and did not catch exactly what she said, what questions might you ask?

1 Because they're not the same blood group as me.

   ....

2 I was going to have to start doing dialysis four times a day.

   ....

3 I was eating my breakfast when the call came.

   ....

4   My friend used to keep a horse 'down the way'.

....

5   My friend had just come round.

....

6   We were about to go out riding.

....

7   I went into hospital on July 16th.

....

8   And it took about ten days for the transplant to kick off.

....

COBUILD CHECK: in hospital

- The following year **he was admitted to hospital** suffering from inflammation of the large intestine.
- Jim will undergo a **minor operation** on his nose.
- A hysterectomy is a **major operation** and is not recommended lightly.
- Muller has been **recovering from** knee **surgery**.
- Laparoscopy is a quick and easy **surgical procedure** which allows a surgeon to look at the internal organs.
- The operation can usually be performed as a **day case,** or at the most needs an overnight stay.

C   Organ donation

In this short extract, Rachael expresses her gratitude to the person who donated the kidney. Listen to the recording. Do you share Rachael's sentiments when she talks about organ donation?

Summarize what Rachael says

1   about how bereaved relatives feel when asked to give consent to organ donation.

2   about why she thinks you should donate an organ to a child who needs it.

3   about how those who receive donor organs feel towards those who have donated them.

Next steps

Both of the native speakers in this unit use an extensive vocabulary and a wide range of grammatical structures. Check the transcripts to ensure you understand the exact meaning of what they say. If you would like to hear more about Oscar's journey and Rachael's full story, go to **www.collinselt.com/englishforlife/extras.**

ANSWER KEY

Unit 1 Everyday travel

A 2

2	1	3	5	4

3

1 He saw a cyclist go straight through a red light.
2 cyclists
3 drivers
4 The idea that drivers pay 'road tax' and cyclists do not. This doesn't make sense as 'road tax' doesn't exist.
5 His religion required him to wear a turban and the helmet wouldn't fit on top of it.
6 Not clearly stated. Mike asks if there is a law enforcing the wearing of hi-vis jackets but Matt says that such a law would be 'a good way to go'.

4

2 b   3 b   4 a   5 b   6 a

5

1 avoid being squashed
2 not enough space
3 can be used
4 free rein
5 a whole rethink
6 with enforcing

B 2

1 b   2 e   3 a   4 c   5 f   6 d

3

2, 3, 6

4

2	reliability	reliable
3	connection/ connectivity	connected
4	transport	transported/transportation
5	unreliability	unreliable
6	order	ordered/orderly
7	lateness	late
8	commuter	commuting

5

1 I guess, I suppose, I think
2 it may be that, perhaps
3 Perhaps, I think, Maybe
4 perhaps, I think, maybe
5 I guess, I suppose, It may be that, Perhaps
6 I guess, I suppose
Note that 'it may be that' cannot be used in sentences 1 and 6

Unit 2 Living with animals

A 2

1 b   2 a   3 b   4 b   5 c   6 a

3

1, 2, 4, 6

4

1, 2, 3, 4, 8

5

1 actually
2 full name
3 build up a relationship

4 completely sulked.
5 what route
6 not looking … sometimes unties
7 grumpy old man
8 ones just left out

B 2

1, 2, 4

3

1b dog tired = exhausted
2g dog-eared = worn, shabby as a result of over-use
3d a cat nap = a short sleep

4e set the cat amongst the pigeons = cause trouble and disturbance

5c let the cat out of the bag = tell something that is supposed to be a secret

6a a catty remark = a nasty comment

7f a dogsbody = someone who does all kinds of unpleasant work

Unit 3   Diet

(A) 2

1 b   2 a   3 a   4 b   5 b   6 a

3

1 d   2 f   3 b   4 e   5 a   6 c

(B) 2

1 T   2 F   3 T   4 F   5 F

3

2 Mould?
3 Yeah that just sounds ridiculous
4 That's … uh.. no, I don't know
5 They say red meat's bad for you.
6 Fish is quite - yeah
7 Yeah that's true.

(C) 2

1 Protein:	meat, fish, eggs, dairy products like milk or cheese
(Vegetable protein):	nuts, seeds, lentils, chickpeas, beans
2 Carbohydrates:	grains – bread, rice, pasta and potatoes
(Complex carbohydrates):	vegetables
3 Fats:	
(Saturated fats):	red meats, dairy products
(Essential fats):	oily fish, salmon, tuna, seeds, avocado

3

1 to make sure you have a good
2 is to think about making sure
3 would be to make sure
4 is the main culprit
5 is made up of

Unit 4   Eating habits

(A) 2

2, 1, 6, 4, 5, 3

3

1 T 2 F 3 T 4 T 5 F 6 F 7 T 8 F

4

1 e   2 a   3 b   4 c   5 d

(B) 2

1 The fact that his British colleagues start eating without waiting and leave the lunch table without giving an excuse or explaining that they are leaving.
2 He would need to excuse himself and explain why he was leaving.
3 He thinks this is rude behaviour and that this is something which would not happen in France.
4 Pudding, especially Christmas pudding.
5 it is not cooked with specific local ingredients or in a traditional way.

3

1 each other
2 unusual and impolite.
3 quite unusual
4 to me it's not a dish
5 specific ingredients

4

	Philippe	'Standard' English (suggestions)
	… people don't wait each other …	… people don't wait **for** each other …
	… before you have even finish your meal …	… before you have even **finished** your meal …
	If I would have to leave the table …	If I **had to** leave the table …
	There's no point to ask permission …	Because there's no point **in asking for** permission
	Now not because I'm used	Not now because I'm used to it.
	Smartphone is very often used during the meals	Smartphones are very often used during mealtimes.

Unit 5   Making arrangements

(A) 2

1 F   2 T   3 T   4 T   5 T   6 F

3

1 like = 8,
2 kind of / kinda = 8
3 say = 4
4 just = 7
5 I guess = 1
6 I suppose = 3
7 I mean = 1
8 you know = 4
9 a bit = 4
10 okay = 2

(B) 1

1 Chloe asks if Grace is 'Mrs' or 'Miss' in her passport. Orlando is mentioned.

2

Grace's date of birth: 9th March 1987
Katie's date of birth: 8th November 1988
Grace's surname: Roberts
Katie's surname: Appleton
Credit card number: 6923 8326 4382 8960
Expiry date: February 2016
Last three digits: 138

Booking reference: 2952453
Departure date and time: 10th August 2013 at 13:00
Hotel in Orlando: Four Points by Sheraton in Studio City
Departure date/time from Orlando: 14th August 08:28
Hotel in Cancun: The Occidental Grand Xcaret
Departure date/time from Cancun: 24th August 2013 at 19:00
Total cost of the holiday: £2798.79

(C) 1

Grace wants to spend another day in Orlando and would like to fly to Cancun in the evening rather than the morning. Jade says it's no problem.

2

1 was wondering
2 just confirm your full name
3 were you looking
4 you're going
5 would probably
6 hour and a half for the flight times

3

Busy hustle and bustle, action-packed, hectic, noisy, crowded, full-on
Relaxed peaceful, lazy, laid-back, tranquil, unhurried, restful

---

Unit 6   Technical help

(A) 2

2 authentication
3 the ethernet cable
4 the address bar
5 the summary page
6 a) green
   b) red

3

1 just confirm
2 what's called
3 just run through for me.
4 what we know from that
5 gonna (going to) talk you through
6 mean by that
7 what I mean
8 need you to type in

9 should be showing
10 does that say anything like your

4

1 Can I take your home telephone number, please?
2 I'm just actually having some problems with my broadband
3 Just tell me what the wording is underneath
4 (so) of you give me a moment, I'll just turn off my Wi-Fi.
5 I'll grab that ethernet cable.
6 So what am I supposed to do now?
7 (so) I've taken that out.
8 I need you to type in all lower-case, admin
9 What should be showing at the moment … is that …

B 1

Sample answers:
1 There's something wrong with the phone screen.
2 The phone is still under warranty, so it'll be sent to a repair centre and the engineer will say whether it can be repaired for free or not.

2

1, 2, 4, 6, 8

3

1 me get your details
2 has been sent out to
3 covered under
4 has been already booked in
5 in the meantime?
6 also been set up

Unit 7   Voicemails

 1

Voicemail 1	c Where are you?
Voicemail 2	e Have a good holiday!
Voicemail 3	d Booking a table
Voicemail 4	b Going to be late
Voicemail 5	a Confirming a reservation

2

(In the author's view, Kerry sounds quite relaxed about the situation.)

Kerry: Hi there. Um, I'm so sorry <u>to miss you</u>. I'm at the restaurant, it's eight o'clock, I thought we were gonna (going to) meet here round now but you haven't <u>shown up</u>, so <u>I'm assuming</u> you're running late. If you could just give me a call, let me know <u>when you think you'll be here</u> … uh … that'd be great. Okay, <u>looking forward to seeing you</u>. Bye.

3

1 She is going to France.
2 After Clare returns from her holiday

4

1 Tonight at 8 o'clock.
2 For six people.
3 She would like someone from the restaurant to call her back to confirm the booking.

5

Sample answers:
1 Just to let you know I'm running late.
2 Been stuck in a jam for half an hour.
3 Not very happy.
4 Be good to talk later.
5 Not going to take the motorway next time.

6

1 a
2 b

3 a (Josh says: 'if the weather doesn't hold out', which implies it is good now).

4 a

B 1

Voicemail 6	c Left something behind
Voicemail 7	f Will send some documents
Voicemail 8	b I was in a meeting
Voicemail 9	d A delayed flight
Voicemail 10	a Think I'm lost
Voicemail 11	e Giving directions

2

1 of six in the corner
2 bracelet
3 by the table, in the ladies
4 silver

3

1 trying to park   3 'll (will) be sending
2 'll (will) send   4 you've got

4

1 I was   c in a meeting
2 Okay,   e lots of love
3 We haven't spoken   d in a while
4 So give me   a a call back this evening
5 Be good   b to have a chat
6 Sorry   g to miss your call
7 Hi,   f it's Katie

5

1 a Dubai
  b The flight is delayed due to bad weather.
2 a My flight has been delayed.
  b I will keep you updated.

6

1	just coming	3	not quite sure exactly
2	a bit	4	could, would be

7

1   She'll reach a flyover
2   A few hundred metres
3   Yes

Unit 8   Registration and induction

A 2

1   6 a.m.–10 p.m.   2   9 a.m.–5 p.m.   3   5 floors
4   4 areas   5   3rd floor, area D. B3D

3

1   in every area
2   every six months
3   in the basement
4   Pilates, yoga or sculpt (note Karolina should have said 'sculpture' because 'sculpt' is a verb)
5   8a.m.–5p.m.
6   next to the shelves in the café area
7   Carl McClarke

B 2

1 T   2 F   3 T   4 T   5 F   6 T   7 F   8 F   9 T

3

1f to sign up for classes
2c to update the system
3a to fill in the accident book
4e to take a shower
5d to inform the switchboard operators
6b to issue security passes

C 2

1   you want to come and register with
2   you're living
3   where you're living
4   to prove to me who you are and where you.
5   you've got a bank statement
6   you've got a utility
7   if I go and copy
8   to stay and help
9   complete that part
10 like to fill in that one

3

1   She cross-checks the patient's address with the practice boundary map to see if the address is inside the boundary area.
2   Yes
3   Three years
4   Kenya
5   Her signature.
6   Yes, she does. She is allergic to an antibiotic.
7   Sixteen years
8   48 hours

Unit 9   Getting along

A 1

Sample answers:

John and Freddy mention the following issues:

keeping outdoor shoes on when inside a flat

choice of food, music or TV

a feeling of being crowded

being grumpy (moodiness)

not emptying the bin

not keeping fixtures and fittings in order (e.g. not fixing the toilet)

'unfair division of labour' (when one person does more work to keep the flat clean and tidy than the others)

2

1 easy 2 argues 3 looking forward 4 refused
5 did all the cleaning

3

… because you've had the same upbringing.	[2]
… they've become firm friends …	[5]
There's more room for disagreeing on how you should live.	[1]
I think people might argue with their siblings.	[3]
… we didn't clash.	[4]
… he had been holding a grudge against me.	[9]
The trick is to find other grumpy people!	[6]
We're all sticklers for principle.	[8]
I'm now fairly intolerant of other people's feelings.	[7]

4

1 f   2 d   3 a   4 g   5 b   6 e   7 c

5

tolerant	intolerant
easy-going	unaccepting
accepting	prejudiced
understanding	biased
unprejudiced	bigoted
sympathetic	disapproving
laid-back	
forbearing	

 1

Sample answers:

1 money: Celia says they are generally compatible when it comes to money and work well as a team (they can rely on each other). Karen simply says that she has a different approach to finance than her partner.

2 driving: Celia implies that there is no problem when she is in the car with her husband, but Karen says that she usually argues with her husband about navigating.

2

1 At work
2 No
3 His proactivity and creativity
4 Partners should have the same moral and ethical values and also, possibly, spiritual values.
5 Finance can be an area of difficulty.
6 In the car
7 Pete
8 He is incapable of following a satnav.

3

1 creative   5 cautious
2 pull him up   6 rows
3 outset   7 swerving
4 compatible   8 backseat driver

4

1 don't we   7 didn't we
2 isn't it true that   8 weren't we
3 tell me   9 isn't it
4 can't you   10 can't we
5 won't you   11 don't you
6 hasn't it   12 Don't you think

Unit 10   Cultural observations

 1

Sample answers:

Lauren says that both in Germany and the US, people go out for 'brunch'. She also says that people in Germany stay out in bars until one or two in the morning, which is similar to what she experienced in New York.

Dieter thinks that 'cross-cultural' relationships are not easy as they create what he calls 'organizational problems'. He enjoys living within two cultures but feels, nevertheless, that a 'cross-cultural' life can be stressful.

2

1 T   2 F   3 T   4 F   5 F   6 T

 1

Sample answer:

In the UK there is no obligation for a person to live with his/her parents whereas in Saudi Arabia you are encouraged to live with them and look after them.

Hussain says that there are male and female sections in Saudi homes and implies that this is not the case in the UK.

He says that boys and girls study separately in Saudi Arabia, which is not the case in the UK.

2

1, 2, 3, 4, 7

3

1 an obligation   5 segregation/separation
2 to come over   6 mentality
3 the norm   7 mixed education
4 elderly people   8 to encounter

C **2**

1 like a code for the clothing
2 modesty
3 some problems with   5 for women here
4 the opposite way   6 if she prefers

3

Standard English *(suggestions)*

there are different attitudes

she has to wear modest dress / she has to dress modestly

certain types of clothing

by the police

on the other hand / whereas

she has to bear that in mind

4

2   You should be given information about local customs by the travel agent

3   You might be asked to take your shoes off.

4   The guidebook must definitely be studied carefully before we leave. You must be offered the opportunity by your tour guide to ask questions.

5   Your car ought to be parked in a secure area at night.

6   You may be fined by the police if you drop litter in the streets.

Unit 11   Social media

 2

1   to keep up / trying to sift through

2   the level of old-fashioned communication

3   statuses on Facebook / tweets

4   care what I say

5   a mobile thing, I think / on the move.

6   run out of lives on my

7   I'm drawn more

8   comes down to, like..

3

1b   2a   3a   4b

 2

Noun	Adjective
obsesssion	obsessed
selection	selective
fun	fun
obligation	obliged
disadvantage	disadvantaged
spontaneity	spontaneous
strength	strong

3

1, 2, 4, 6, 7

4

1b   2a   3e   4c   5f   6d

 2

1   A picture, her Twitter name (Rachworld) and the fact that she comes from the Lake District.

2   They Tweet about things such as what they are having for breakfast.

3   'Humble bragging': in other words making their lives sound better than they are.

4   Famous people / well-known people

5   Retweets of other people's Tweets. She resends other people's Tweets.

6   28

4

1   I've heard that   4   it's all

2   wants to know   5   not always

3   on Facebook   6   it really takes

Unit 12   Attitudes to work

 1

Sample answers:

Karen says that when she lived in Sweden, she felt the society there had a good balance of work and leisure.

Celia agrees with her and says that when she lived in Sweden, the company had shorter working hours in summer and longer hours in winter to maximize the amount of daylight.

Karen worked six days a week and long hours in Hong Kong, but she also had a very active social life.

When Karen moved to Singapore, she very often travelled with her job. As she also had a young family, this was a challenging situation for her.

Both Karen and Celia agree that business trips sound glamorous, but are actually very tiring.

2

1 T   2 F   3 T   4 F   5 T   6 T

3

1a   1b   2a   3a   4a   4b

4

Negative	Positive
tough	flexible, glamorous *fabulous*
disillusioned	
exhausting	
unsettling	
wearing	

5

2   Gosh!

3   That was tough?

4   It's exhausting, travelling, isn't it? (It sounds really glamorous and I think for a short …)

5   It's quite unsettling, isn't it?

6   That's really tough, yeah.

B 1

Sample answers:

In Austria, Eva had a very short journey to work – only 5 minutes walking or cycling. In London, she has a longer commute. Consequently, her working day in the UK is longer and she has less free time.

Work starts later in London than in Austria.

Eva implies that Austrians have a good work/life balance, but that Londoners prioritize work over family or social life.

2

1   on foot or by bicycle

2   by bicycle or on the Tube

3   an hour by bicycle or 45 minutes on the Tube

4   Everything starts later; she can start work later in the morning

5   It is somewhere between what she describes as the Italian 'live to work' attitude and the German 'our life is all about work'.

6   What do you do for a living?

3

1,2,3,5,8

4

1 commute   4 the Tube

2 walkable   5 an early riser

3 cyclable   6 prominent

Unit 13   Charities

A 2

Sample answers:

1   She wanted to do something more worthwhile and suddenly her father died. She realized that 'life is short' and that she needed to take action before it was too late.

2   Because of financial considerations. She needed to pay her mortgage.

3   She resigned from her job and began working as a volunteer with Macmillan.

4   She loves her job.

5   It is known for its specialist nurses.

6   The grants it gives to people who need money.

7   A female cancer sufferer who needed money so she could visit her son and a father who needed to fund a Christmas party for his family. Macmillan may also buy wedding dresses or washing machines – anything that people suffering from cancer may need.

8   A cancer patient received an 'all-clear' – the good news that the cancer was no longer present in her body. She wanted to thank them for supporting her during the time that she had the illness.

3

1   put things into perspective

2   resigned

3   to volunteer

4   just go for

5   grants

6   supporters (and taking) donations

7   to have a Christmas party

8   support line

9   really touched

10 got the all-clear, and you helped me

4

1   put in perspective   5   be cured

2   be fortunate   6   be touched by

3   be mad   7   get money

4   go around to people   8   get the all-clear

B 2

1   to be touched by   5   publicity

2   a massive number   6   to sign up

3   good outcomes   7   sob stories

4   the appropriate charity   8   worthwhile

3

1 T 2 F 3 F 4 F 5 F 6 F

4

1D 2S 3S 4S 5D 6S 7S 8D 9S 10S 11D

5

Sample answers:

1 Because of his own experience with his father and the fact that you cannot give money to everything.

2 He does not like this approach and ignores them.

3 She says that she hates them and that they make her feel bad.

Unit 14   Collecting

(A) 2

silver, tea caddies, paintings, auctions, car-boot sale, antique centres, furniture, nice objects, treasures

3

1	a passion for	4	to have a passion
2	specialize in	5	passionate about
3	great fun	6	try to get

4

1 passion *passionate*
2 collection *collectible*
3 antique *antique*
4 *exuberance* *exuberant*
5 treasure *treasured*
6 *enthusiasm* *enthusiastic*
7 preoccupation *preoccupied*
8 *fanaticism (or fanatic)* *fanatical*

(B) 1

Raphaël's collections: cards with bird pictures, postcards of castles, film posters, stamps, trainers, mobile phones

2

1 b   2 d   3 a   4 b   5 b   6 a

3

1 C   2 S   3 S   4 S   5 C
6 S   7 S   8 C   9 C   10 C

(C) 2

1 He was around twenty years old
2 To try to cure his bad handwriting
3 Pens that were made in the 1920s or 1930s. =
4 Five to seven pens
5 Thirty to forty pens
6 A Japanese pen (with a special nib)

3

1 relatively inexpensive
2 led to
3 envy
4 particularly attractive
5 was intrigued
6 I'd invested in
7 was taking more – paying more (*note how David corrects himself*)
8 prized possession

4

1 My handwriting was always very, very poor.
2 a relatively inexpensive fountain pen
3 I started to develop fountain pen envy.
4 I'd invested in these pens.
5 There's an American brand called Parker.
6 I don't display them in a glass case.
7 My prized possession.
8 It has really exquisite details on it.

Unit 15   Music

(A) 1

Zhang talks about a rock band called Tang Dynasty and Wang says she is too young to remember them.

2

1 T   2 T   3 F   4 F   5 T   6 F

3

1	alone	4	popular
2	last	5	band
3	elements	6	mainstream

4

	Verb	Adjective	Adverb
1	to perfect	*perfect*	*perfectly*
2	to strengthen	*strong*	*strongly*
3	to sooth	*soothing*	*soothingly*
4	--- (no verb)	particular	*particularly*
5	to prefer	*preferred*	*preferably*
6	to notice	*noticeable*	*noticeably*

 B **2**

1, 3, 4, 8

3

1 aspirational thing
2 evolved over
3 replicate
4 you don't get to see all
5 fan following
6 released

4

1 celebrating
2 evolved
3 addressing
4 replicate
5 crazy about
6 pastime
7 evolution
8 simultaneously

Unit 16   Environment

A **1**

1 The discarded fishing nets are converted into carpet tiles.
2 It can last for up to six hundred years.
3 The term 'ghost-fishing' is used to describe the situation when discarded nets continue to catch and kill fish and other marine life in the sea or on beaches.

2

Sample answers:

1 Net-works recycles old fishing nets and turns them into carpet tiles.
2 Nylon has many uses. It can be used to make carpet, fishing nets, computers and car tyres.
3 Fishermen throw their nets away after 2–3 months (after they have become damaged and cannot catch fish as effectively).
4 They tend to dump their nets on local beaches or in the sea.
5 It reduces the volume of fish local people are able to catch. This means that local people earn less money from fishing. Additionally, ghost-fishing contributes to the problem of overfishing and has a negative impact on fish stock levels.
6 They collect the old nets from fishermen before the fishermen throw them away. They also collect discarded nets from beaches. They then clean them before they sell them to the Net-Works organization.

3

1 really exciting initiative
2 are damaged and ripped
3 last for up to six hundred years
4 heavily, heavily overfished
5 are — are completely dependent
6 community-based supply chains
7 groups aggregate   8   only recycling plant

4

1g	2b	3h	4f	5a	6d	7e	8c

B **3**

Sample answers:

1 Five or six containers
2 Dead batteries, plastics, vinyl and paper.
3 They may be given a warning or a fine.
4 People must pay for the amount of food they throw away. To reduce the cost, people try to throw away less food. The smell of food waste has also become an issue.
5 They have to measure the amount of CO_2 every household consumes.
6 It is to raise their awareness of how much CO_2 we produce.
7 It can help us to reduce the amount of CO_2 we produce.

4

Order in which phrases are used:

1 … the most commonplace environmental effort …
2 … five different categories …
3 … a big collection point …
4 … sometimes you can be fined …
5 … the machine actually weighs the food waste …
6 … everyday household effort …
7 So there is a school assignment about CO_2 reduction
8 I think we can actually reduce the amount of CO_2 we produce

Unit 17 Weddings

 2

Sample answers:

1   for a couple of days at least / several days.
2   Most are arranged weddings.
3   Jewellery and clothes
4   The costumes, culture, ceremony and amount of time the ceremony takes differ.
5   In the north of India, the groom's family typically organizes a reception.
6   Seven to eight hundred.
7   They can be a terrible waste of food and money – especially given the poverty which exists in India. He implies that something better could be done with the food and money.
8   No, poor families also spend more than they can afford on family weddings.

3

1   are arranged
2   a one-day affair
3   celebrations happening
4   a huge affair
5   hosted a lunch
6   bless the couple
7   tend to waste a lot of
8   you can actually afford

B 2

Sample answers:

1   They're fine. (going well)
2   In three weeks' time.
3   The bridal party walk through the ceremony so that everyone knows what they are going to be doing on the day of the wedding.
4   The night before the wedding.
5   She isn't very enthusiastic about the rehearsal dinner as she wants the focus to be on the wedding day rather than on the night before the wedding day.

6   The bride and groom feed each other a piece of wedding cake.
7   Patrick (the groom), Nikki's dad, all of the wedding party, the ushers and quite a few of the guests.
8   No, they won't, because Nikki says the family tartan isn't very nice.
9   They see it as a fun thing to do. Often they will never have another chance.
10 Very successful. She thinks it will be 'fantastic'.

3

1   a wedding reception (or a wedding ceremony)
2   (the) best man
3   stag party
4   the guest list
5   The bride and groom
6   my mother-in-law-to-be (or my mother-in-law)
7   maid of honour
8   hen party, (or bachelorette party)

4

1   rather frightening
2   it's just strange
3   things that I expected
4   an important thing in America
5   a kind of rehearsal

5

1   must be
2   been to one
3   actually involve
4   might help anybody with cold feet
5   really make an entrance
6   what I think is the most important
7   about your family
8   it'll be fantastic

Unit 18 Rising to a challenge

 1

Sample answers:

Walking along a jungle trail and walking on a beach at night.

2

Sample answers:

1   It was her last (exciting) holiday (last hurrah) before she had children.
2   The jungle was filled with enormous spiders; they didn't know whether the spiders were deadly or not.

3 They wanted to experience different foods and have a walk on the beautiful, deserted beach.

4 Because they can open coconuts with their claws.

5 They hurried (scurried) back into the jungle.

3

1 h great fun
2 g a final good experience
3 f a near escape
4 d risk everything
5 a totally dark
6 b absolutely everywhere
7 e understand something after a bad experience
8 c very relaxed

4

1 the size of my head
2 was filled
3 had to duck
4 emerge and take over
5 their huge claws
6 scurry
7 complete terror
8 hilarious

 2

2 very muddy   5 wanted to
3 unaffected by   6 sad
4 badly   7 more comfortable

3

1 festival-goers
2 The weather was just about OK.
3 it just got ridiculous
4 random things
5 to bump into
6 the rain was tipping down
7 keep trucking
8 to go 'glam' camping (glam = glamorous)

4

1 cannot / could not be flooded
2 in an extremely clean condition
3 the rain was pouring down / it was raining very hard
4 to walk with difficulty in a very heavy, slow way (used when walking through mud, sand or snow across difficult ground)
5 crowds all gather around
6 take down / take apart
7 extremely hard
8 the mud left a lasting, even damaging impression on her (a rather strong use of the word 'scar'!)
9 the brief period when an opportunity exists
10 to insist upon / to be very keen on (to be a stickler for something is to be someone who insists on things being just as they want them to be)

Unit 19   Holiday destinations

A 2

1, 2, 5, 9, 10

3

Sample answers:

cutting-edge = very up-to-date, very new

bouncer = person who is employed to maintain security and order and can remove someone from a building or event (bounce them)

cove = small bay on the coast

jetlag = tiredness and sense of disorientation caused by flying across several time zones

coastal route = road which sticks close to the coast so that travellers can see the sea

boiling = very hot

koala bear sanctuary = place where koalas are protected and looked after

pouch = the bag which marsupials have in which they carry their babies

tame = not afraid of and friendly towards humans

shade = protection from the sun afforded by, for example, a tree

joey = a baby kangaroo which is old enough to walk/jump itself

4

1 cute   5 amazing
2 cutting edge   6 glamorous
3 boiling   7 lovely
4 tame   8 cosmopolitan

5

1 b   2 b   3 a   4 a   5 a   6 b

1

Sample answers:

1 She says that the weather is not good in August. It is very hot and very humid. She does not like the weather in August because it is 'very sweaty and sticky'.

2 It is a huge festival which is held in Japan in August. During the festival, people pay their respects to their ancestors. Shops often close for three days during the festival.

2

Sample answers:

1 You can experience the Obon festival.

2 Shops tend to close and this could cause inconvenience.

3 More in rural areas.

4 No, they don't. They have never lived outside their 'home town' (which is not identified).

5 The 13th August is the first day of the festival and so most people go to a shrine and pray to their ancestors.

6 People go to the shrine again.

7 A traditional Japanese costume which is similar to a kimono.

3

1 … someone who is from Tokyo …

2 If you go to rural areas …

3 Then we have a traditional meal …

4 So, it's more like a religious thing to me …

5 You can really enjoy wearing it. / It is really nice/ enjoyable to wear.

6 So it looks like a kimono, but it's much lighter …

Unit 20   Life-changing events

A 1

Sample answers:

--Oscar sailed from the last island in the Canaries (the race actually starts from Las Palmas de Gran Canaria) to the island of St Lucia in the Caribbean.

--He enjoyed the isolation most, being completely alone at sea.

--Yes, he would recommend anyone to take part in the race.

2

1 Atlantic Race for Cruisers

2 A hurricane

3 Force 6–7.

4 Yes, he did.

5 A satellite phone

6 A sextant and a chart. Also a GPS system, but it was not always available.

7 No, he wasn't.

8 The sun sinking into the sea.

3

1 I took part in

2 are measured

3 such large sailing ships

4 head on into

5 come and pick you up

6 would have been

7 start to work out

8 plotting it

9 hadn't done

10 au fait with (to be 'au fait' with something means to be fully informed about something or be familiar with it – the expression comes from French)

4

1 to take part

2 a voyage

3 the Beaufort scale

4 the isolation

5 faint lights

6 to pick you up

7 at its zenith

8 the skipper

9 to get to know the ropes

10 to be au fait with what was going on

B 2

Sample answers:

1 They are not the same blood group.

2 Because he is younger than her.

3 She was eating a bowl of Cheerios and was about to go out riding with a friend. (Cheerios = a breakfast cereal)

4 Twenty minutes

5 One day

6 She felt much better – full of life and full of energy.

3

1 Why couldn't your parents donate a kidney?
2 Sorry, how many times a day?
3 Sorry, what were you doing?
4 Where did she keep the horse?
5 Who had just come round?
6 What were you about to do?
7 When did you go into hospital? / Sorry, when did you say you went into hospital?
8 Sorry, how long did it take? What do you mean by 'kick off'?

C 2

Sample answers:

1 She empathizes with bereaved families and can understand why they might not consent to a donation.
2 Because when you have died you do not need it any more.
3 She thinks anyone who has received an organ will always be grateful to the donor.

The transcript below is an exact representation of what each speaker on the *Listening* CD says. No corrections or adaptations have been made.

Unit 1   Everyday travel

Track 01

Mike This morning I saw a cyclist go straight through a red light and I feel they have a complete disregard for the laws of the road.

Matt No, I agree with you. Cyclists should never jump red lights, they should never disobey the laws of the road, but there's always more to it than that, I think. A lot of the time a cyclist will feel in danger and feel that they have to cross a red light to a— avoid being squashed by a car. I think it's more important— I mean, maybe if there were cycle paths everywhere, then— then it would be different.

Mike I feel like in this city there's not really enough space for the cycle paths. Like, the— the roads were built a long time ago, a lot of them, and there's just— they're— they're very narrow, so there's not enough space to have the cycle lane, the bus lane and then the regular lanes for the cars.

Matt Yeah, of course. I agree. A lot of the time cycle paths actually make cycling more dangerous, because I think they give cyclists and road u—...uh...drivers the idea that cyclists should only be in the cycle lane. Now, cycle lanes can be used but you don't have to use them as a cyclist.

Mike So a cyclist doesn't have to be in the cycle lane if he doesn't want to be? I didn't actually know that.

Matt No, I don't think so. As far as I'm aware the— the cyclist ha— can choose to be in the cycle lane or not. The cycle lane is a guide to the driver I think, as far as I'm aware.

Mike Som— something else that bothers me is that I always hear...um...cyclists say that buses— or— or bus drivers and taxi drivers think they own the road. [*Yeah.*] But I definitely think it's the other way round, that cyclists feel that they have complete free— free rein of what to do out on the roads – they're completely in charge because they're the most vulnerable.

Matt Yeah. I think it's a really difficult relationship and I think a lot of myths have sprung up around it. Um, I cycle and quite often you will get bus drivers who act aggressively to cyclists as they wouldn't do if I was in a car. So for example, if I'm coming up on the right side of a bus and it suddenly starts indicating, it'll start to pull out on me if I'm on a cycle— if I'm on a bike. But if I'm in a car it won't do that. I mean, for example, your example of who owns the road. I was cycling once and got cut up by a car driver and I went to the window, had a conversation, at which point the...uh...female passenger pointed to the road tax disc and said, 'we pay for the road, you don't'. And there's not much you can say about that, there's not much you can say to argue with that. Apart from the fact that actually, road tax doesn't exist. There's never been anything called road tax. We— we all pay through our taxes for the roads.

Mike So you are paying, then?

Matt No, we're all paying

Mike Yeah.

Matt Yeah, but it's not just the car drivers who are paying. They— there seems to be this idea that car drivers and anyone who uses the road in— on a powered vehicle pays for it and the cyclists just use it free of charge. It's just not the case. As long as you're paying taxes, we're all paying for the same thing. I think actually there needs to be a whole rethink…um…behind the whole process, and that— I think we all need to think about not just who owns the road and who has right of way and stuff, but actually get back down to what the roads are for and how we should drive, how we sh— we should respect each other on the roads, not just if we're pedestrians or car users or lorry users or— or cyclists, but actually how everyone uses the road which is a bit more respectful to everyone else.

I think legalizing helmets could be an interesting path that we go down. A lot of old-school riders won't go with it because they've never done it – they don't see it's something they should do. And one of the arguments is that…uh…s— car drivers seeing a cyclist without a helmet will drive more carefully around that cyclist. Um, it's been used in Australia…uh…and in Australia it's illegal to ride a bike without a helmet. But then again, that brings its own things— there's never a cut and dried rule. Apparently a Sikh gentleman was recently given the right in Australia to ride without a helmet because it wouldn't fit on top of his turban. Now, you're always gonna get sort of…uh…things which you can't enforce to the full degree, and it's all about, sort of, having a little bit of common sense in some issues I think.

Mike Do you wear other protective clothing [*Yeah, well—*] or just a helmet?

Matt I think it's always important to try and be seen. You should have lights but a lot of people don't around London, and you see a lot of people just riding around. Y— I— I'll miss them. So you look down the road and you don't see someone until they're very close to you because they're riding all in black and they haven't got lights on. Uh—

Mike Perhaps they should introduce some sort of law that—

Matt Well, the laws are there. It's just about enforcing them.

Mike Oh, there is a— there is already a law about [*Well, lights.*] wearing hi-vis and …?

Matt Well, maybe hi-vis would be a good way to go as well…um…just to sort of— just to make everything seem a little bit fairer. But again, there are always gonna be difficulties with enforcing something like that.

Track 02

Neeraj Today is actually the second day that we're here and coming into the office. It's a lovely walk, not too far from the office, takes us about five minutes, whereas in India where we live you have to commute and it u— it will usually take about an hour to get to the office. We have to…uh…drive through a lot of traffic. And…uh…my colleague here, he lives quite close to the office but still…uh…because of the traffic he t— he— he ends up…uh…taking as much amount of time as I do.

Krishna Uh, commuting in India is a big—…uh…big issue. Uh, it's pretty chaotic, there's a lot of traffic, too many cars…uh…and without a sense of direction, there's no lane driving there, so we end up spending, like, an hour or so every day commuting. Uh, that's the minimum that people do. Some— some cases people spend more than two hours one way to come in to office and two hours to go back. So— but here in the UK it's…uh…it's much more simple, I guess. Uh, people do spend a lot of time but…uh…they take— take tube or— or…uh…maybe some of them drive on their own. But I think…um…there is much more semblance here. People stick to the lanes, and…uh…there's no pressure driving. Uh, I think so.

Neeraj Yeah, and also people are…uh…much used to using the public transport here, whereas we rely mostly on our own…uh…mode of transport. We use our own cars wherever we need to go.

Krishna Uh, that's— that's mainly because we don't have a proper public transport system. Uh, but there's buses or the tube…uh…the— the connectivity is not very good so people rely on their own…uh…transport…uh…on their own cars or motorbikes.

Unit 2   Living with animals

Track 03

Ian	So— so how's— how's the horse?
Fiona	It's actually a pony, Ian!
Ian	Is it?
Fiona	Yes. I've actually got a New Forest pony.
Ian	Have you?
Fiona	Which is native to the United Kingdom. [*Right, okay.*] Yeah. 'Cos it's like a moorland horse.
Ian	A moorland horse – what's that?
Fiona	Well, you know, like Exmoor – all the different counties we have in the United Kingdom.
Ian	Right. And how long have you had her? [*Him.*] Him.
Fiona	Bertie. Actually, his full name is Rushmore Bertie Wooster on his passport.
Ian	He's got a passport?
Fiona	All horses in England have to have passports now, by law. Proper passports, like we do for travelling overseas.
Ian	But does he travel overseas? Have you—
Fiona	No. But by law you have to have a passport in the United Kingdom. [*Okay.*] And that's whereby the vet will come along, draw a picture of your horse, mar]— with all the markings. Every time you have an injection—
Ian	Dra— Draw it?
Fiona	Draw it.
Ian	Right, okay.
Fiona	So you didn't know that?
Ian	I didn't know that. No, no, no.
Fiona	So you've learnt something today.
Ian	I have— I have learnt something, yeah. Yeah. And— and you said that Bertie was very upset when you got back from America?
Fiona	Oh, yes. I went to America for a month and … um … I've had him for eleven, twelve years now [*Yeah.*] and the longest I've probably been away from him is two weeks. So you build up a relationship when you're going down five, six times a week, feeding them, riding them. Especially winter, summer, going to see them in the field. So of course I left him for over four weeks and when I got back he was in his stable and … um … he didn't look at me for two days, turned to the back of the stable, his back to me, and just wouldn't look at me for two days and completely sulked. And also had lost in the last two weeks— probably lost a stone, two stone in weight. And the vet reckons that he was pining for me [*Mhmm.*] which kind of shocked me in a way because I wasn't used to that— that we'd built up that kind of relationship.
Ian	Yeah. So are all— all horses like that? Is that normal?
Fiona	I think they are, because they do rely on human beings. [*Mhmm.*] And they do trust. It's all about trust as well. They don't— For example, if I go out for a ride on the lane, and I— I might do the same route two or three times a week, and— for example, one day last week there was a massive log just lying in the middle of the lane, which is not normally there, he— he would just spook at that. It's like what— He would get agitated by it. Why is it there?
Ian	How strange.
Fiona	Yeah, and they remember things as well, they remember what route they go on, and what things that have annoyed them in the past, and they just— they remember things.
Ian	So you can tell whether Bertie's in a good mood or a bad mood or—

Fiona	Oh, completely. Totally. I mean, this is the cheeky chappy that if he has the farrier coming to do his shoes— new shoes, which is ever—
Ian	Sorry, what's a farrier?
Fiona	A farrier is like a traditional blacksmith. [*Right, okay.*] that— that— So every eight weeks they get new shoes, so they can go out on the road, [*Mhmm.*] so it doesn't get their feet sore. But…um…for example, he— he— he hates the farrier, or he's very cheeky with the farrier. So when the farrier's not looking he sometimes unties all the ropes of the other horses that are in line waiting to have their feet done. So he's— he's very much like a naughty teenager from school. [*Mhmm.*] So they do have their traits. And then other days he's like a grumpy old man, not eating his dinner. And then other days again he's just like a five-year-old child going a hundred miles an hour round the fields that you can't stop. It's just— you just don't know from one day from the next what mood he's gonna be in.
Ian	So it's not to do with his diet or what the weather's like or—
Fiona	No. Well it can be— it can be the change— a change in weather is a major factor definitely. [*Yeah.*] Definitely.
Ian	Yeah, okay. And are they all like that— are all horses— they've all got different personalities, have they?
Fiona	Yeah, they all have. But I do find that the ponies, the smaller ones, are a lot more intelligent than your big shire horse [*Right.*] in that sort of way. And we've also got a donkey on the farm that's a complete psycho so…
Ian	In what way is it a psycho?
Fiona	He's just very noisy, very— just— I don't know, I just don't think— B he doesn't get ridden and you do find that the ones that are getting ridden all the time are probably got— getting more attention [*Yeah.*] 'cos they're being groomed, they're having dinner after they come back from their ride, while the ones just left out in the field, they must just get bored. I would!

Track 04

Um, also…uh…the idea that— some Muslims…uh…that they—…uh…they religiously are not encouraged to— to…uh…touch dogs, especially the— the— the mouth of the dog. So…um…this is…uh…something to expect when you come to England, that people will bring their dogs, and in many cases dogs are regarded like one of the family. So…uh…you will find it quite a lot in— in people houses so don't be surprised when— when you see that. And feel free to— to express what you think about that.

And…um…the same thing…um…apply to— to anyone…um…who— who…um…may go from England or from Britain to Saudi Arabia and he…uh…wish to— to bring his dog with him. It's not common in— in Saudi Arabia to— to see one is walking his dog. Um, you will find— you will find the dogs are just …uh…um… walking by their—…um…themselves. No-one really, in— except in few cases that— for example, for— for herding or for guarding, some— some people would keep dogs but it's not the common perception in here or the common idea in— in Britain where people will have their…uh…dogs live with them in the— the house. It's completely different in— in Saudi Arabia. So this is something also t— to bear in mind.

Unit 3   Diet

Track 05

Freddy	So I hear you're a vegetarian?
Lily	Yeah.
Freddy	Ah, interesting. I've got a friend who…uh…has just decided to become a vegetarian.
Lily	Oh really?

Freddy Yeah— no— I don't understand it. I think it's a fashion statement or something.

Lily A fashion statement?

Freddy I can't— Why else would you become a vegetarian? I mean, why do people do it? Why?

Lily Well— I suppose at the moment there seems— it seems to be quite trendy to kind of be [*Exactly.*] healthy, like it's healthier, especially with, like— there's been a lot of talk in the newspapers about where meat comes from and what's in the food that we eat and stuff so I suppose if you're a vegetarian you know— it's a lot easier to know what's in the food that you buy.

Freddy Yeah, I think she's just doing it because…um…she just wants to impress artists, probably greengrocers.
I don't— you know— I've— I've never understood. I mean, don't you miss meat? Have you ever eaten meat?

Lily Well, not really. I can't really remember the last time I ate meat. I was probably three or four years old, [*Ah. So*—] I was really young.

Freddy Are your parents vegetarians?

Lily No, that's the strange thing. Um, I'm the only one in my family who's a vegetarian. Um—

Freddy And you became a vegetarian at three?

Lily Well, basically, I think— I— I've met a couple of people in my life who have had the same story as me so I know I'm not the only one, but I think when I was younger…um…I just never really liked meat so I never chose it, or if it was an op— if I had a choice, I'd just— I would always prefer to have something vegetarian.

Freddy Really?

Lily Yeah. And my parents kind of noticed that I never really liked it, so—

Freddy What about hotdogs?

Lily Well, when you're three you don't really eat hotdogs.

Freddy I— I think I ate hotdogs!

Lily Well I didn't! Um, but we ate a lot of…um…things like chicken and fish in our household – we didn't eat a lot of red meat anyway. So if I went to a friend's house and they were having burgers or whatever, I mean— I'd eat it [*Ah.*] because I had to but I never really wanted to.

Freddy So you don't really know if you like meat? [*I suppose so…*] I mean, if you haven't eaten it since you're three…

Lily Ah, well the thing— this is what happened. So, I never really liked it as a child, and then my older sister – she's about five years older than me –…um…she…um…decided to become a vegetarian because— but for different reasons. She was very—…um…she didn't like the idea of eating meat and— and killing animals for our food and things like that so she went vegetarian for that reason, so she was …um…

Freddy She's more of a ethical vegetarian.

Lily Yeah, but still, she was really young to make that decision at that age. [*Uhuh.*] Um, and so I copied her. Part— part of it was I copied her, and then part of it was— it was easy to copy her because I didn't really like meat anyway. So that's— I think that's essentially how it happened.

Freddy But what— I mean, don't you … Well, I always think— I mean vegetarians must be— you must be quite a, I don't know, kind of lackadaisical, overly-relaxed— you must be missing a lot of energy in your life. I mean, meat – you need it for everything, for getting on a bus to waking up in the morning. I mean, meat gives you the energy to do that.

Lily Okay, I get on the bus in the morning, I wake up every morning and I don't eat meat.

Freddy But I mean, it must be a real struggle for you, I imagine.

Lily It's not at all. I— I suppose the only— I don't feel like I have any less energy and I don't feel like I'm at any disadvantage to anyone else but I suppose the main problem would be if you go to— if you're on holiday, if you're in another country where there's not a lot of vegetarian food…um…or when you go round to someone's house…um…and they've cooked something really—

Freddy Yeah, I mean, I would never, ever cook— I mean, I wouldn't— I'd obviously offer my guests meat. I mean, I don't want to—

Lily Well, that's the thing. When people come to my house, I don't know how to cook meat, so they have to eat vegetarian food. Um, ... but when I go to— if I go to someone's house and they've made a real special effort to cook something nice and they've spent a lot of time and money, then it is really, really embarrassing when you have to sort of say, I— you can't eat it, c— 'cos I really can't, like, I— I won't eat it. There has been times when I've had to out of politeness, but that's mostly— When I've given in it's mostly been about fish and seafood and things like that when— and— and that has— over time that's now— it's actually changed so I now eat fish, and the— the only reason I eat fish really is because I've been in situations where I've felt like I had to. Um, or in a lot of countries— I mean, for example— Spain is a really good example. Um, if you ask for something vegetarian, generally they— they count— well, in my experience, they count things like fish as vegetarian. So over time, I've— I've started eating fish and I love fish. So who knows, maybe one day, if I ate some more meat ...

Track 06

Lily Yeah, I think a lot of the time it's about having some inspiration for what— like, g— good ideas for what you could cook and do with vegetables. And also, don't forget, it's not just about vegetables. If you're a vegetarian, you might eat— there's things like Quorn and all sorts of things.

Freddy Uh, what's Quorn?

Lily You know, like, that stuff you— it's like ... um ... it's a kind of protein, it's like a meat substitute. I think it's made from ... um ... almost a fungus. I know that sounds disgusting [*Oh, yeah, mmm.*] but it's grown, and it's got the texture of— it is— it's actually quite nice. It's got the texture— [*Mould?*] apparently it's got the same texture as chicken or similar. So a lot of people who maybe don't eat meat for health reasons ... um ... but they miss the taste of meat ... um ... might eat Quorn. That's not what I do 'cos I don't miss the taste of meat, but I can see why—

Freddy Yeah, that just sounds ridiculous.

Lily Um, yeah— no— well, you can get, like, for example, you can get Quorn in different shapes and things so you could get Quorn mince and you could use it as a replacement in food like lasagne where you might want it instead of having minced meat. So all I'm saying is, you— there's a lot you can do with vegetarian food beyond just boiling [*That's ... uh... no, I don't know.*] vegetables.

Freddy I think a balanced diet— [*They say red meat's bad for you.*] I think maybe we eat too much meat as a country and definitely, like, it's easy to eat— it's easy to eat very unhealthily and eat a lot of meat. But I think a balanced diet is what you should have. I mean, I think humans are naturally omnivores, aren't we?

Lily Yeah, I agree, but I— like, now, I find ... um ... it's a lot cheaper to eat ... um ... to not eat meat as often. Like, I find even buying fish a few times a week is quite— is— has increased my food bills like quite a lot [*Fish is quite—yeah.*] But it's— I really like it now and I can see— it's a lot easier to plan meals around having not just vegetarian food. Cause also, with veggie food, you have to— you have to— it— sometimes you have to cook quite a lot more to bring the same flavours [*Yeah.*] and to have that amount of variety.

Freddy What, with vegetables?

Lily Yeah, [*No— yeah, I think so.*] like when I eat fish, I can cook some fish and have vegetables on the side but to come up with an idea for a vegetarian dish takes a lot more.

Freddy Yeah, it takes a lot more.

Lily So maybe just— meat eaters are just lazy.

Freddy Uh, I think maybe— I think— yeah, I think— it's— it is— yeah, it's interesting that— I think if you want to eat cheaply you probably do end up eating quite a lot of meat, unless you're a really good cook and know how to cook vegetables because, like, cheap food in the supermarkets will tend to be kind of processed meats and stuff, or I find... [*Yeah, that's true.*] or maybe that's where I'm looking. Whereas, yeah, with vegetables you have to know the recipes, you have to maybe go to a grocer's, like, a second shop, yeah. Yeah— no— maybe— maybe it's a— maybe it's just Britain at large. It's our diet.

Lily Yeah. I think in— and it depends as well. Like you said, in China they eat more vegetables, but…um…it depends where you are.

Freddy Yeah, they can— they know how to— they just know how to cook vegetables, whereas I only ever got taught how to cook lasagne, roast chicken—

Lily Ah, maybe you just need cooking lessons, then.

Track 07

The right nutrition is absolutely vital for good health, and in terms of the right nutrition it means a very varied and balanced diet. There are three main food groups: protein, which is made up of foods like meat, fish, eggs, dairy products like milk or cheese, and then vegetable protein with things such as nuts and seeds, lentils, chickpeas, beans. The next major food group is carbohydrate, which is often made up of grains, so things like bread, rice, pasta…uh…also potatoes. And…uh…there's a section called complex carbohydrates which includes vegetables. And then the third section is fat. And fat breaks down into two sections: saturated fats, which tend to be found in…uh…red meats or dairy products, for example, and what we call essential fats, which are the Omega 3…um…essential fats, which…uh…there's been a lot of advertise and marketing around these days, and they tend to be found in oily fish, for example – salmon or tuna…um…seeds, avocado, etcetera. Now, it's very important to make sure that you have a blend of each of those different nutrients – protein, fats and carbohydrate – because they each play a very different role, and an important role, for the various bodily functions. If you don't get enough of one of them, then there will be a knock-on effect, which may ultimately lead to some kind of health problem. If you get too many of one, the same kind of thing can happen. So it's very important to make sure you're having a good balance of all three.

On top of that, we have something called micro-nutrients, and these are made up of vitamins and minerals. They're equally important. They contain things like vitamin A, vitamin C, and minerals are things like calcium, iron, magnesium, etcetera. Each of these…uh…in small quantities are very, very important for health and so it's important to make sure that you're eating plenty of the right foods. In terms of how to approach this, the best thing first of all is to think about making sure that you're having a good balance of protein and carbohydrate with every meal and snack. The best way to go would be to make sure it's complex carbohydrate, and that's what I like to call brown foods – things such as brown bread, wholemeal bread, gr— granary bread, or bread with seeds. Um, also brown rice or whole-wheat pasta. Other great examples of— of complex carbohydrates are all the different kinds of vegetables. Now, if you blend complex carbohydrates with protein, then that's going to lead to sustained energy, and for those people who feel tired all the time or who have those energy dips – for many of us it's at three o' clock in the afternoon where it's very hard to get back to work – it's usually because you haven't had enough protein at lunchtime and it's also usually because you haven't been eating the right kind of carbohydrate.

When I talk about the wrong kind of carbohydrate, what I basically mean is sugar. Sugar is a major problem at all kinds of levels. First of all, sugar is the main culprit when it comes to weight gain. Everybody thinks about fat, but poor old fat needs a new PR company because actually the f— the reason it's called fat is not because it makes you fat. Fat does not make you fat, sugar makes you fat. And sugar can be found in so many foods. Not just the obvious things like chocolate or cakes or cookies, but also…um…the— the white foods, the white carbohydrates, so white bread, white rice, white pasta and lots of refined foods. So if your lunch is made up of a white bread sandwich and a bar of chocolate, then what will happen is your body will burn through that very, very quickly, and you'll end up with this famous energy dip in the afternoon. If you have, for example, a brown bread sandwich with a good quantity of protein in the form of, let's say, chicken or salmon, and maybe a piece of fruit, then you're going to be getting fibre and protein all in one go. Fibre, which is complex carbohydrate – another word for complex carbohydrate if you like – is very, very important because it's slow-release energy. Protein is hard to digest, so it slows down the release of the carbohydrate even further. So if you can think about having protein with every meal and snack, you are much more likely a) to have sustained energy levels throughout the day, and you won't be relying on the coffee or the chocolate all the time, and secondly, you're going to be— you're much less likely to be putting on weight, which is always a bonus for most of us these days.

Unit 4   Eating habits

Track 08

When they have a dinner, they— all family should be together … uh … especially kids doesn't start meal without their mum, without their dads, because … uh … es— especially some real— really traditional … uh … families. Uh, first of all, mum and dads start— … uh … they start eat, then kids start to eat. Uh, but you know, it's old-fashioned way. Uh, but usually in that— generally … uh … all family should be together, especially at dinner. Uh, they eat together and … uh … they finish it together. Uh, if they finish early, no one leaves the table. They gonna sit and they gonna eat, they gonna finished and … uh … when they're in table the Turkish people love the speaking, and they are talking about what they— what did they do that day, blah blah blah, like that. And soup, salad and rice. They're, you know … uh … always has to be there in the table.

Uh, and I was living in Black Sea side— I am living in Black Sea side … uh … and there is— … uh … chicken dishes are really popular in … Black Sea side, and fish. Uh, there is sea basses and anchovies, yes, is the most popular fish in Black Sea and especially in winter … uh … almost everyone out there eat fish.

Uh, but when we are talking about … uh … restaurants and family homes in Turkey … uh … it's— not completely, but it's a bit different. Uh, here's some particular foods Turkish mothers do … uh … generally. And— … uh … for example, rice. Most of people rice is very famous in China but it's not like that. Um, in Turkey, every night— almost every evening, I'm sorry— every evening … uh … it's— in the kitchen there has to be rice and salads … uh … with main dish. Uh, Turkish people use rice … uh … as a side order. And before— before— before the main dishes, actually as a starter, every Turkish home— Turkish house, there has to be soup. Generally it is lentil soup. They— all families start their meal … uh … with lentil soup and … uh … esp— especially kids, if they don't eat soup, the mother's … uh … pushing them and they has— they have to … uh … eat soup firstly. It can be lentil or yoghurt soup … uh … and then they can … uh … start with their main course.

Track 09

Philippe Lunch is really, really different. Really different. Um, people don't wait each other— each other to go for lunch. Uh, people start their lunch … uh … without … uh … waiting colleagues to start their lunch the same time. They would leave the table before you have even finish your meal, without excusing at all— without no reason at all, so that's quite … uh … astonishing for me, from— … uh … from a French guy, that I am.

Ian Do you find it rude?

Philippe Now not because I'm used. But the first time I— I— I— I felt it was huge.

Ian Yeah. So what would you do? You would always say 'excuse me' or what?

Philippe Yes. [*Yeah.*] Yes. Most of the time I wouldn't do that, unless I have a strong … uh … a— a— a strong commitment or a strong … uh … excuse or strong … um … reason to leave the table before the others and if— if I would have to leave the table before the others I would excuse myself and giving the reason of why— of my leaving. Um, one of the difference as well is that now that every person has a— smartphone, so smartphone is very often used during the meals. Uh, people, once they have finished their lunch, even if they are lunching with other people, with colleagues, they very often … uh … use a mobile phone … um … browse the Internet [*Uhuh.*] even if you are in front of them. So that's quite unusual and quite impolite. This sort of thing would be quite impolite in France.

Ian Okay, so— so people wouldn't do that in France?

Philippe No. No, that's quite impolite, I would say.

Ian Right. Or they would have to ask for permission, if you like, to do something or they just wouldn't do it?

Philippe Even not, even not. There's no point to ask permission to— to browse Internet and to use mobile phone when— when you are lunching.

Ian Yeah. Are— are there any … uh … English dishes which you like from a— from a French point of view that you've thought 'I've never had this before in France and I really like it'?

Philippe I like the … um … the puddings. [*Mhmm.*] And the Christmas pudding, yes, I like it. [*You like that?*] I like it a lot. [*Okay.*] I know that most French people don't like that much but … uh … I like it, yes … uh … yes. Uh, in terms of dishes, I wouldn't say that fish and chips is dishes— is a dish.

Ian So you don't like fish and chips, do you?

Philippe I don't say that I don't like it, but to me it's not a dish. It's just fish with— with chips, why we say that— that it is a dish?

Ian Okay. So— so you like fish? [*Yeah.*] But not British fish and chips?

Philippe I do. Uh, no, I do— I do like it. [*Yeah.*] But we would say a— about a dish that it is … uh … a specific traditional meal because it's— the way it is cooked, it is cooked with specific ingredients from … uh … that are— locally typical, etcetera, etcetera. Uh, what is typical in fish? What is typical in chips? There's nothing typical.

Ian Yeah.

Unit 5　Making arrangements and changes

Track 10

Chloe Thank you for calling Virgin Holidays, Chloe speaking, how can I help?

Grace Hi. Chloe. Um, I'm interested in booking a holiday to Mexico for about probably fourteen days, and I just wanted— I thought that maybe you could give me a bit of advice?

Chloe Yeah, course. So firstly, have you been to Mexico before?

Grace I haven't, no.

Chloe Oh, okay. I've actually just returned from Mexico and it was … uh … wonderful, so good destination, tick. It's a lovely— … uh … lovely place [*Yeah.*] to go to. So have you, like, looked at any hotels or got anywhere in mind that you wanted to stay, or just open to, kind of, recommendations?

Grace I'm definitely open to recommendations. Um, I suppose I'm interested in seeing the city and … um … maybe going to the beaches as well, if that's possible? I'm not sure how close by they are to the city. [*Yeah.*] Um—

Chloe Yeah, so that's definitely a possibility. So … um … I stayed … um … when I went there at … um … a, Occidental property, and that was only … um … like, an hour away from, say, Cancun. So what a lot of— like, what we did and what a lot of other guests that we kind of made friends did … um … they booked … uh … trips to either go back into the city or to see, kind of the, more original, authentic side of Mexico … um … 'cos you're not that far away. So they kept themselves at one hotel rather than— as it's only, like, an hour away, rather than, you know, doing say, a few nights in one hotel in the centre of the city and then moving. But, it's up to you. If you wanted to do, say, two different hotels you could do, but because you're only kind of like an hour transfer away, what a lot of people did was did, like, day trips and went back into the city. But it's to— totally up to you, [*Oh.*] what you'd like to do.

Grace Yeah. No, that sounds perfect. Um, 'cos it'll just be myself and one friend [*Okay.*] … um … so we'll be travelling together. And … um … is it easy enough to organize transport back to the city? Do the buses run regularly and everything?

Chloe Yeah. When we were there we did it … um … a few different ways. So, like, one time we just got a taxi that we organized ourself, and it was quite reasonably priced. Another time we did, like, scheduled transport, so something that was pre-organized with other people, and that was very kind of seamless as well. So I— I would say that would be the best way to do it. Um, and also [*Okay.*] it's a bit more relaxing, I guess, 'cos you can get to the hotel on the first night, unpack, you know that's where you're gonna be, but you know that you're gonna be going out for, like, days at a time, you know. So that— I thought that was better. So if we're looking at the hotel, what do you kind of go for in a hotel? What— what is it that you— what's important to you?

Grace I suppose because there's just two of us we'd … um … like to stay somewhere where we'll hopefully meet people our own age [*Yeah.*] Um, maybe somewhere with a pool. And, yeah, just lively but not too noisy, I suppose [*Yeah.*] would be perfect.

Chloe Yeah, no worries. So Mexico is … um … quite a lively place, I would say. Um, we— we definitely— there are hotels that are obviously focused on, say, just spas or real relaxation. Um, but where we went to … um … it was lovely, because they played, like, music round the pool. I mean, not like booming, you know, club— nightclub music or anything like that but … um … you know, it was just— it was a bit more relaxed whereas— they had a lovely pool bar that you could go and swim up to and you met … uh … other people, and there was a bit of music there, so it was a bit more relaxed. So … um … yeah, I— we've definitely got something that kind of could— could meet that— that, definitely. Yeah. [*Yeah.*] Now, what … um … dates is it that you were looking to travel?

Grace Um, it would be August. So it would be … um … probably the 10th of August until the 24th.

Chloe Okay, I'll take a little look at what days they fall on. Now, we don't fly every day to Mexico. I believe we fly … uh … Saturdays, Tuesdays and Thursdays. So I'm sure [*Oh I see.*] that we'll be able to kind of fit that in. So what I'll need to do first of all is just take some details from yourself to set us up on your system. So … um … can I take your name, please?

Grace It's Grace [*Grace.*] Roberts.

Chloe Uh, Grace Roberts. Okay, Grace. And if you didn't catch my name again, it was Chloe, okay? [*Great, thanks Chloe.*] Um, Grace, what was your postcode, please?

Grace Um, I don't actually have one because it's Ireland – we don't have postcodes.

Chloe Oh, okay, no worries.

Track 11

Chloe Would you like us to go ahead and get that booked up for you?

Grace Yes, please.

Chloe Fantastic. So I'll need to take everyone's names and dates of birth as per passport. So, Grace, is it Miss or Mrs on your passport?

Grace Miss.

Chloe Perfect. And can I take your date of birth, please?

Grace The ninth of the third, eighty-seven.

Chloe Wonderful. And your friend, what was her name, sorry?

Grace Um, Katie.

Chloe Katie, was that, sorry?

Grace Yep. So that's K-A-T-I-E.

Chloe Wonderful. And what was her surname?

Grace Appleton.

Chloe Appleton. Wonderful. And Katie's date of birth, please?

Grace Um, the eighth of the eleventh, [*Yeah*] eighty-eight.

Chloe Did you forget then?

Grace I did for a second!

Chloe And then you think, 'I'm such a terrible friend!' [*Yeah.*] So what I'm gonna do is just phonetically read them back to you and make sure we've got them all correctly. We have to have them as per … uh … your passport, otherwise … uh … they obviously don't let you check in, 'cos it has to be the same on the ticket as it is on the passport. So Grace, we've got yourself, and that's … uh … G— G for golf, R for Romeo, A for alpha, C for Charlie, E for echo. And I've got Roberts, that's R for Romeo, O for Oscar, B for Bertie, E for echo, R for Romeo, T for Tommy, S for sugar. And that's the ninth of the third, nineteen eighty-seven. [*Okay.*] And then I've got your friend as Miss Katie, and that's K for kilo, A for alpha, T for tango, I for India, E for echo. And it was Appleton. A for Alpha,

P for papa, P for papa, L for lima, E for echo, T for tango, O for Oscar, N for November. And she was the eighth of the eleventh, nineteen eighty-eight. Was that all correct?

Grace Yes, good, perfect.

Chloe Fantastic. So what I'll need to do now is just take the long number on your credit or debit card? [*Okay.*] So how're you— was it a credit or a debit card that you were looking to pay with?

Grace Um, it's a credit card.

Chloe Lovely. So just to let you know, we do charge a surcharge on a credit card of three and a half per cent, okay?

Grace Yep, that's fine.

Chloe Lovely. When you're ready with that long card number, then, please.

Grace So it's 6-9-2-3 [*Yeah.*] 8-3-2-6 [*Yeah.*] 4-3-8-2 [*Yeah.*] 8-9-6-0.

Chloe Yeah. Wonderful. And the expiry date on that.

Grace The second of 2016.

Chloe Wonderful. And the last three digits on the back of the signature strip?

Grace 1-3-8.

Chloe Fantastic. Right, that's just going through now. [*Okay.*] Lovely, that's gone on to the booking, so that is all paid for and booked. You are going on holiday!

Grace Brilliant, thank you so much [*So let me just give you—*] for your help, Chloe.

Chloe That's alright, let me give you that booking reference. [*Okay.*] So the booking reference is 2-9 [*Yep.*] 5-2 [*5-2.*] 4-5-3. [*4-5-3. Okay.*] That was 2-9-5-2-4-5-3. So what I'm just gonna do is just check everything and confirm everything with you once more, 'cos I'd hate for you to kind of go away and everything not be booked…uh…kind of perfectly, okay? [*Okay.*] So I'll just recap everything with you, if that's okay. So we have you guys travelling out on Saturday the tenth of August 2013, we've got the V-room booked for you before you travel. The flight departs from London Gatwick at 1300 and arrives into Orlando at 1705. Then we've got you staying for four nights at the Four Points by Sheraton in Studio City, then on the 14th of August departing from London— from, sorry, Orlando at 0828 and arriving into Cancun at 0921, staying for ten nights at The Occidental Grand Xcaret from the 14th to the 24th, and then on the 14th— on the 24th, sorry, departing at 1900 and arriving in at 1010 the following day. [*Okay.*] And then that's for— all of those travel components are for two passengers, and the total cost of the holiday is 2798 and 79p. Was that all correct?

Grace It was.

Chloe Fantastic!

Track 12

Jade Hi, you're through to Jade McEwan in customer services, how can I help?

Grace Hi Jade. Um, I made a booking yesterday…um…with your colleague Chloe. It's for a trip to Mexico and Orlando, and I was just wondering if I could make a small change to one of the flights.

Jade Absolutely, yes. Do you have your booking reference number there?

Grace I— I do. It's 2-9 [*Yeah.*] 5-2-4 [*Yeah.*] 5-3.

Jade Wonderful. Okay, I'll just bring that up for you. And…uh…with— just with data protection, can I just confirm your full name and your postcode, please?

Grace Yep. So my name is Grace Roberts, [*Yeah.*] and…um…I don't have a— have a postcode but my address is…um…5 Doyle Road, Dublin.

Jade Yeah, that's wonderful. No, that's absolutely perfect. And I have your itinerary from— starting from the tenth of August, off to Orlando, and then on to Cancun. [*Yes.*] Um, so how can I help? Which— which part of the holiday were you looking for?

Grace Um, well originally I booked the flight, I think it was for the morning to fly to Cancun, and I was wondering if I could change that for a later flight so that we would have another full day in Orlando, and maybe…um…to spend a bit more time at the parks or something.

Jade Yeah, of course, yeah. 'Cos I can see you're going at…uh…half past eight in the morning [*Yeah.*] so…um…would you prefer to go, like, about six o'clock or would you like an evening flight [*I—*] to be transferred over?

Grace Um, did you mean six o' clock in the evening or—?

Jade Yeah, yeah, like…uh…evening time or— or we could do later. We're very flexible.

Grace Um, I think six would probably be a good time so it's not too late then when we're— when we arrive in Mexico. What time would it be— if— if we left Orlando at six, what time would we arrive in Mexico?

Jade Um, it would probably be about quarter to—…um…quarter to nine. [*Okay.*] It looks like it's only— I'll have a look for you anyway. I'll just double-check now. [*Okay. Thank you.*] Um, but it's only an hour and a half…um…for the flight times anyways. So have you been to Orlando and Cancun before or is this your first time out there?

Grace It's our first time.

Jade Oh wonderful, wonderful. It's quite a nice mix 'cos you're kind of busy in the city— oh, or— well, in Orlando, just in the parks, you're always hustle and bustle and running around, and then you've got the relaxation of the beach so it's…um…it'll be so nice [*Yeah.*] to mix them up. The …um—

Grace We're really looking forward to it.

Unit 6   Technical help

Track 13

Liz Good afternoon, welcome to TalkTalk. You're speaking to Liz. Can I take your home telephone number, please?

Jay Hi, good afternoon. Yes, my number is 0-2-0-8 [*Yeah.*] 3-0-7 [*Yeah.*] 4-7-double 1.

Liz Thank you very much. And c— can I just confirm who I'm speaking to this afternoon please?

Jay Sure, my name's Jay, my surname's Ali.

Liz Thank you Mr Ali. And how can I help you today? You're speaking to Liz.

Jay Um, I'm just actually having problems with my broadband. It's not connecting. I'm not sure why.

Liz Okay. Um, first of all, can you see the router at the moment?

Jay So wha— what would the router look like?

Liz Right, the router is…uh…the main kit that you plug into your telephone line. So you will have, from your telephone line, …uh…your telephone plugged in and what's called a router. Do you understand what I mean?

Jay Is— is— is— is that, like, the box with the lights?

Liz That's correct, yes.

Jay Okay. Yes, I've got that here.

Liz Right, so you can see it at the moment. Right, I'd like you to just run through for me what lights you've got on at the moment. So starting say from left to right, just tell me what the wording is underneath, and what colour the light is, or if it's on or off.

Jay Okay. So, from the left there's the power light, which is green [*Yeah.*]…um…so I think it's turned on. Um, next to that there is…uh…another— another button…um…and that's red, and I think— I don't know if that's maybe upstream, and then I've got one next to that and then that's green…um…that's the downstream. And one next to that.

Liz Okay. So the green light, does it say anything like DSL or ADSL at the side of it [*Yes, it does.*] or is it just a symbol? It does say ADSL. And the— the one that's red, does that say Internet at the side of it?

Jay Yes, it does. I think I just read it wrong, [*Okay.*] I think. That says Internet.

Liz Yep. Okay. Alright. So what we know from that is that the signal between the exchange and your router is solid, but you're not getting what's called authentication, which means that you're not getting on to the Internet. Um, the information that's…uh…being passed to the exchange is either incorrect or there's— there's a problem…um…with that equipment. So we just need to work out exactly what's causing that. And the way we need to do that is by accessing into the router. Now don't worry, I'm gonna talk you through that. [*Okay.*] But first of all, are you using a laptop or a desktop?

Jay I'm using a laptop.

Liz A laptop, okay. And are you connected in a wired state? What I mean by that is, is there a cable that runs— an ethernet cable that runs from the router to your laptop?

Jay Uh, no. I'm using wireless.

Liz Wireless. Do you have an ethernet cable available to you?

Jay Uh, yes I do. [*You do. It's just*—] Do you want me to plug that in?

Liz Yes, please, 'cos it's just simpler to connect to the router itself in that instance.

Jay Okay, so if you give me a moment I'll just turn off my Wi-Fi and I'll grab that ethernet cable.

Liz Thank you.

Jay Um. Okay, so I've turned off Wi-Fi and I'm just plugging in the cable. And I've plugged that in. [*Okay.*] Um, so what am I supposed to do now?

Liz Right, okay. So what I want you to do— Don't worry that we've not got an Internet connection on this, but we just— I just want you to open an Internet Explorer page as normal. It will come up [*Okay.*] 'page cannot be displayed'.

Jay Yes, that's came up. And it's still not working so it says 'page cannot be displayed'.

Liz Okay. Do you know what I mean by the address bar? It's right at the very top of the page, where it says http?

Jay Okay, yes, I've found that.

Liz Okay. Um, I want you to delete anything that's in that box so that there's nothing in the box, please.

Jay Okay, so I've taken that out.

Liz Okay. Um, I want you to type in 1-9-2-dot.

Jay 1-9-2. Do I need to put in the http part? Do I just delete all that?

Liz Uh, yes, delete everything, so there's nothing at all in that box.

Jay Okay, so I'll take that part out as well. [*Okay.*] Okay, so what— can you just repeat that, it was 1-9?

Liz 1-9-2-dot [*Uhuh, 1-9-2-dot.*] 1-6-8-dot [*1-6-8-dot.*] 1-dot-1.

Jay 1-dot-1. And just press enter?

Liz Press enter, please. [*Okay.*] It's then gonna present you requesting a username and password, [*Okay, so I can't remember what my*—] you tell me when you see that. Well, no, but this—

Jay Uh, I can see that but I can't remember my—

Liz Okay, don't worry about that, 'cos this is just a generic username and password to access into the router, this isn't your username and password. Okay? [*Yeah.*] Um, so in the username, I need you to type in all lower-case, admin, A-D-M-I-N.

Jay A-D-M-I-N. Uhuh. And in the password field?

Liz And— and the password is exactly the same, in lower-case, admin.

Jay Admin as well.

Liz Yeah. And then it's either 'okay' or a connect button.

Jay Okay, that's 'okay'. I've just pressed 'okay', [*Okay.*] and I think that's logged into the page.

Liz Alright. You'll probably open on what's called a summary page. On that it should show you— Um, on the left hand side, you should have … uh … three— three circles, colour coded, one that says DSL, one that says Internet, and one that says wireless.

Jay Yeah, that's correct.

Liz Okay. Um, what should be showing at the moment, from the information you've given me, is that the … um … ADSL light and the wireless light would be green and the Internet light is on red. Is that correct?

Jay Yep, that's correct, yes.

Liz Okay, just at the side of that box, towards the right hand side of those lights, there will be the username and password. Now, does that say anything like your home telephone number as the username? [*Uh.*] Or does it just say— is it blank or does it say— … um … [*It—*] it— it can sometimes say where, how, or something like that, or blank, or— it's starting with your home telephone—

Jay It's just blank.

Liz It's blank. Right, okay. Alright, so what's happening is, the router is not sending any information to the exchange so it's not recognizing who you are.

Track 14

Megan Hiya. I've bought a phone here … um … a couple of months ago. [*Okay.*] It's stopped working – I think the screen's— the screen's— sort of, if I press one area it'll— [*Okay.*] the mouse'll come up on another bit.

Nixon Okay, so basically you have issue with your screen on your phone. Uh, do you bought it from Carphone Warehouse?

Megan Yeah.

Nixon Okay, do you have your mobile with you now?

Megan Uh, yeah.

Nixon Okay. Okay, that's fine. Uh, let me get your details up here. [*Thanks.*] Okay, so your name is Megan, right? [*Yeah.*] Okay, Megan, so what would you like to do? Do you have insurance on the phone?

Megan Uh, no I don't have insurance [*You don't have insurance.*] but I think it should still be under its guarantee, so—

Nixon You got it under warranty. Okay, what we can do— … uh … we got a separate— Not in our store, but we got separate … um … repair centres. So I can book in for repair, which you don't need to pay for it. [*Okay.*] So when the phone has been sent out to the repair centre, the engineers will have a look for you, and then he's gonna find out whether— if it's something cover under the warranty. If it's covered under the warranty, you don't need to pay for it. It takes up to two to three weeks time, so mobile to be fixed and sent out to the store. [*Okay.*] You can come and collect here. If not, the engineer will let us know the chargeable repair. Or— so if it's a chargeable repair he will let us know the amount that you need to pay in order to get that … uh … phone fixed. If it's something that's chargeable then we'll contact you [*Okay.*] and I— as soon as you're happy to pay for the— the repair … uh … then he will fix it and send out to us. So you come to the store, you pay for it, you collect it. Would you like to go ahead with that?

Megan Okay, yeah, that's fine, yeah. Thanks.

Nixon Okay, so let me get this updated on the system, so give us one minute, okay?

There, so it's all done. Um, so your mobile has been already booked in for repair. I just need to get you to sign for this, please. Would you please sign for it?

Megan That's fine, cheers. Um, [*Yeah?*] will I get a temporary phone in the meantime?

Nixon	Yes. Uh, yeah, I'll give you a temporary phone so it's so we have a very basics temporary phones only. Uh, so that's the temporary phone for you. [*Okay.*] Do you want me to put the— in the SIM card and everything set up for you?
Megan	Uh, yeah, would you mind?
Nixon	Uh, yeah, so your phone has been— your new phone has also been set up so everything ready to go and up and running. Uh, so all you need to do is just wait for us to give you a call. [*Okay.*] Uh, the phone that I just gave you is basically— if you … uh … fail to bring it back as it is, we charge you fifty pound for it. [*Okay.*] As soon as you bring it back in, we'll give you the new phone. As soon as your phone is fixed, everything is ready, that's it ready, [*Right.*] all ready to go, okay? [*That's great, thank you.*] Happy to go with that?
Megan	Yeah, thank you.
Nixon	Alright, cheers. Thank you.
Megan	Cheers.

Unit 7   Voicemails

Track 15

Voicemail 1

Hi there. Um, I'm so sorry to miss you. I'm at the restaurant, it's eight o'clock. I thought we were gonna meet here round now but you haven't shown up, so I'm assuming you're running late. If you could just give me a call, let me know when you think you'll be here … uh … that'd be great. Okay, looking forward to seeing you. Bye.

Track 16

Voicemail 2

Hi Clare, it's Grace calling. I just wanted to have a chat with you before you go to France next week. Um, just wanted to say have a great holiday and I'll talk to you when you're back. Bye.

Track 17

Voicemail 3

Oh, hello. I was wondering if it was possible to book a table for tonight. Uh, it's a party of six and we would like to come at eight o'clock. Uh, my number is 0-7 […] 2-7-8. Would be great if you could give me a call back to confirm. Thanks. Bye.

Track 18

Voicemail 4

Hi. Just letting you know I'm running a little late. Encountered quite bad traffic. Um, you can order me a drink if you like. See you.

Track 19

Voicemail 5

Hi Mr Smith, it's Josh calling here from The Red Lion … uh … to confirm your booking for twelve people tomorrow night. Um … just in case … uh … the weather doesn't hold out, we've got good forecasts … uh … we've … uh … reserved you a table for twelve outside and twelve inside … um … just to be sure. Thanks very much and … uh … we'll see you tomorrow.

Track 20

Voicemail 6

Hi there. I ate in your restaurant last night. We were the table of six in the corner. I might have left…um…my bracelet behind. It could be by the table or in the ladies or something. It's silver with charms. Could you let me know? My name is Mirka and my number is […] 2-1. Thanks. Bye.

Track 21

Voicemail 7

Hi Virpi. It's Teresa. Um, sorry I missed you. Um, I was just trying to park my car. Um, anyway, I'll send you…um…the update later…um…and I'll be sending you some other documents to go with that as well. Anyway give me a ring if you've got any questions.

Track 22

Voicemail 8

Hi, it's Katie. Sorry to miss your call – I was in a meeting. Um, be good to have a chat, we haven't spoken in a while, so give me a call back…uh…this evening. Okay, lots of love. Bye.

Track 23

Voicemail 9

It's Layan calling. Uh, my flight been delayed so I had to wait in Dubai to change planes. Apparently the weather's too bad. Uh, I will let you know anyway, keep you update. Bye.

Track 24

Voicemail 10

Hiya. Uh, I'm just coming by to view your house. It's Eva speaking here. Um, I'm on my way but I think…um…I'm a bit lost. I'm not quite sure exactly if I'm on the right road. Um, if you could give me a ring back that would be great. I'm on…um…0 […] 5-8-9.

Track 25

Voicemail 11

Hi, sorry I missed your call. Uh, it sounds like you're just near the station. Uh, if you just follow the road in front of you straight across…uh…you'll come to the flyover. Just go under the flyover, over the next road, follow it along for a few hundred metres until you can see the bridge, follow the— follow the road along to the bridge, over the river, and we're just in front of you on the left.

Unit 8   Registration and induction

Track 26

So if you don't mind— well, let me just start by giving you some information about the building. The…um…opening times are 6am till…um…10pm. That's…uh…only…uh…Monday to Friday. Saturdays, Sundays and bank holidays it's 9am till 5pm. Um, as far as the building structure goes, the whole building is called Block B. Um, we have five floors. Each floor is divided into four areas – A, B, C and D. It's quite important that you know your location, 'cos whenever you contact facilities to report, let's say, a flickering light…um…basically, it would be good if you know— if you knew your location 'cos that way it's easier for us to find you in the building. Um, so at the moment we are on the third floor in D area, so our current location is B3D.

Um, we have a kitchen in every area. There are toilets next to the lifts … um … and there is one fire exit in each area. Let me just show you one as an example. Uh, right, so the fire exits are clearly marked. The fire alarm test takes place every Monday at 8.30am. There is a list of fire marshals in every kitchen … um … and on the intranet as well. We also do a six-monthly evacuation exercise. Um, the last one was in May so the next one'll probably be sometime around August or October.

Um, now let's go to the café. It's on the ground floor so we will have to take the lift. Uh, we also have … um … squash courts, I'm not sure if you're aware, in … um … basement— in the basement, level minus 2. Um, to book them out you basically have to get in touch with … um … reception at West 6, which is the building just in front of ours. Um, and they are actually quite cheap 'cos it's 3 pounds 25 pence for 45 minutes, so it's not that bad. Um, they don't provide racquets, though, so … uh … if you play squash, basically you have to bring your own racquet. But there is an option of … um … signing up for a different classes like pilates, yoga or sculpt. Um, they take place during lunchtime … um … in the squash courts, and I think yoga is on Tuesdays, pilates on Wednesdays and … um … sculpt on Thursdays.

Right, so this is the café area. The opening times are … um … 8am till 5pm. Uh, they have an ATM, free of charge, just next to the shelves, and they serve breakfast, lunches and snacks. Um, there is also a hospitality booking form … um … which can be found on the intranet, and once filled in it's processed by Carl McClarke, who's the hospitality manager. Um, if you have any queries with regards to hospitality, ordering stuff, etcetera, you can always email Carl or just give him a buzz and he'll be able to help. Um, right, so we're done here. And … um … the next stop is the post room.

Track 27

So … um … this is the post room. The internal mail collection times are 9.30, and the next one is at 11.30, next one at half past two and the very last one at half past three. Um, if you have a large amount of printing, you can always contact Lester Roberts … um … who will be able to help you with … um … whatever you need. Basically, everything that's over 100 pages should be sent to the rep— reprographics room and … um … Lester should deal with it. Um, also if you need your documents to be bound, he's the best person to talk to. Um, if you require a courier service, the post room can be contacted before 5.30. After 5.30 it needs to be reception. For any lost, no-name or missing parcels, the best thing to do is to check the intranet first. If you won't be able to find that information over there then you can always contact Vincent Jordan, who's the post room manager. Um, and there is also a handout which we give to every new starter. It's basically some more information on how the post room and reprographics room work.

Um, now, every person who is staying with us for six months or longer … uh … needs to have their photo taken 'cos we issue security passes for them. Um, work experience people, they—… uh … since they tend to stay with us for only two weeks or less, basically they never give— get passes. But … um … Ron Oakes is the person who normally … um … programmes them and takes the photos as well. All the photos also go onto the intranet, which is the internal database. So…

This is the … um … main reception. Anita is a receptionist and Kwadwo our security guard. Um, Anita is the best person to talk to with regards to … um … booking taxis or flower orders. All the relevant booking forms can be found on the intranet and once filled in have to be returned to Anita so that she can process them. Uh, there is also possibility of borrowing a bike from us. The bikes are in the basement … uh … you need to sign in and out, obviously. Um, we also have four showers behind reception. The reason why we talk about showers is because people actually sign up for the classes which I mentioned – pilates, yoga, etcetera – so it's good to take a shower afterwards or beforehand. Um, again, for the keys, you just have to sign in and out … um … so that's how it works. There are also towels in the showers area so you don't have to bring your own towel, basically. Um, right, so the next stop would be facilities.

So this is the facilities department. Um, that office over there belongs to Anna Storan who's the facilities manager. Um, Anna is actually the best person to contact with regards to … uh … parking requests 'cos she controls the parking. Um, I'm— I'm Anna's PA, I can help with currency requests and I can also help you to … um … sign up for some magazines, newspapers, etcetera. Um, Basia is our helpdesk operator so if you have any issues, but nothing that relates to IT or HR, she's the best person to contact … um … and she should be able to respond quite quickly.

We also have two maintenance guys, Leo and Kerguis, and they basically help with all the minor and bigger jobs … um … in the building. Uh, Mauricio is our cleaning supervisor but we have Karolina covering him today. Uh, we also have two switchboard operators, Ola and Ayesha … uh … which actually brings me to another point. Whenever you change positions … um … or extension numbers we also ask that you email facilities helpdesk or the— or the ladies on the switchboard directly just to inform them about the change so that we can update the system and transfer the calls correctly.

There is also a first aid room just next to the facilities department. Um, there is a first aid— well, accident book actually that needs to be filled in whenever an accident happens. Um, also your line manager and facilities have to be informed if you have an accident at work. Um, all the list of … uh … first-aiders is available in every kitchen as well and on the intranet. Um, as a very last thing that we normally ask every new starter to do is to sign an induction safety checklist. All the information that is on the checklist is in fact in the facilities welcome pack. Um, so yeah, that's more or less the end.

Track 28

Receptionist	Hello Mrs […].
Patient	Hello.
Receptionist	Now, I understand you want to come and register with our GP practice? [*Yes, yeah.*] Is that correct, yes?
Patient	Yes.
Receptionist	First of all, can I check that you're living in our practice boundary or our practice area, please?
Patient	I live in Whitchurch.
Receptionist	And which road?
Patient	27 […] Close.
Receptionist	Lovely, I'm just gonna go and check that on my practice boundary map. [*Okay.*] Thank you.
Patient	Alright.
Receptionist	Right that's lovely, Mrs […], you're within our area. [*Yes.*] Now, I need you to prove to me who you are [*Yes.*] and where you live. So I understand you've got a bank statement there?
Patient	Yes, I have.
Receptionist	Could I look at that, please? Thank you. I also understand you've got your passport? [*Yes, yeah.*] Can I take a look at that? Thank you. And I also understand you've got a utility bill— a bill? [*Yes.*] Wonderful. Do you mind awfully if I go and copy it? [*Yes, you can, yes.*] Thank you. That's fine, thank you. Everything's in order, everything's fine. Now I need you to complete two registration forms [*Yes.*] for me. Would you like me to stay and help you?
Patient	Yes, please.
Receptionist	Lovely, there we go, and there is a pen. That's right, that's your surname, your address and I also need postcode, [*Yes.*] I need the details of your last GP – your last doctor [*Yes.*] – and where you lived before here. And I also need postcodes.
Patient	Okay. In UK I was in Rochdale [*Okay.*] for three years. Before that, I was in Kenya. I came from Kenya.
Receptionist	Wonderful.
Patient	Yes, and I born there as well.
Receptionist	Do you mind me asking awfully what year you came into the UK?
Patient	It's 1960.
Receptionist	Lovely. Could you complete that part for me? Thank you. And the most important thing with anything, signature on the bottom, please. [*Okay.*] Now, because you're coming to us and we haven't got your medical records yet, [*Yes.*] we know nothing about you. [*Okay.*] I need to know a little bit of history about your health – how you are, especially if you're allergic or have reactions

	to any medication, any tablets? [*Yes.*] Okay. So if you'd like to fill that one in for me. I also need an ethnic origin as well, please.
Patient	Okay, I'll put British Asian. I think that's the best thing.
Receptionist	Okay. That's fine.
Patient	There anything else?
Receptionist	And I also need the whole truth and nothing but the truth – if you smoke and how many units of alcohol— how much you drink per week.
Patient	I don't smoke and I don't drink. If I just put nil, [*That's*—] is that okay?
Receptionist	Yeah, yeah, just put nil.
Patient	Anything else?
Receptionist	If we could turn over and fill the back part in, please. Just roughly how much exercise you take? Walking?
Patient	S—…uh…twice a week, I walk to the local shop.
Receptionist	Okay, if you'd like to pop that on there. [*Okay.*] And any drug allergies that you're aware of, that you know about.
Patient	Yes. Is one of the antibiotic I'm allergic to. I can't remember the name now.
Receptionist	Okay. Would you have it written down anywhere? 'Cos it is quite important.
Patient	No, I haven't. I have to look in my diary when I go home and see which drug it is.
Receptionist	If I give you my telephone number, could you ring me?
Patient	Yes, I will.
Receptionist	Thank you. And also just a little bit of your family history. [*Mmm.*] Your parents, your mother, father, perhaps any siblings which are your brothers, sisters.
Patient	Yes. Uh, we got asthma run in our family.
Receptionist	Asthma.
Patient	Yes. I got— my sister and my brother's got that. And high blood pressure, my mum suffered with a high blood pressure, and I suffer with a high blood pressure as well for the last sixteen years.
Receptionist	Okay, if you could complete that for me, please.
Patient	Okay. Yep. Anything else?
Receptionist	That is absolutely everything. Thank you so much. You'll be registered with the practice after forty eight hours, [*Yes.*] after two days. [*Yes.*] But I would like you to telephone me in, there's my telephone number, with what antibiotic you're allergic to.
Patient	Alright. Okay, I will.
Receptionist	That's lovely. Lovely to meet you, Mrs […]. Thank you.
Patient	Okay, thank you very much. Thank you.

Unit 9　Getting along

Track 29

Freddy	Um, I've never— I dunno— I—I've— I live with my brother at the moment so …um…
John	How is that?
Freddy	Well, it's working well. Uh, I think— I think, because we're brothers, we were brought up living the same way and have the same expectations of …uh…how messy things can be, [*Oh, cleanliness. Yeah.*] which are really low, but we share them together. So …uh…there's rarely— there's rarely any arguments. Whereas …um…when you live with people who aren't your brother …um…it's

maybe more fun … uh … in some ways, but … uh … yeah, y— I think there's more room for disagreeing on how— [*Yeah.*] how you should live.

John I found the same thing. I lived with my brother and … uh … and it was the same. I think because you've— you've had the same upbringing and you've been through the same things, you— you … um … you have the same standards and— and you like the same food [*Yeah.*] and the same music and the same TV so it all— it all fits into place quite nicely. I do know a lot of people who've said they would never live with siblings.

Freddy I think— yeah, I, y— I think— 'Cos other people— I think people might argue with their siblings. But I luckily don't argue with my brother.

John Oh, we argued. [*Ah.*] We argued a lot but you know, we— we always argue anyway so it didn't really make a difference whether we were living together or not. [*Right, yeah, yeah.*] Yeah, and as you say, we didn't have the same— we didn't live the same life so we didn't see each other too much, [*Yeah.*] we didn't clash.

Freddy No, me and my brother don't— don't argue. We're very passive aggressive really, I think … But yeah. No, but I— I'm gonna move out of living with my brother to go and live with … uh … two of my friends who … um … I lived with for four years when I was at university, so … um …

John So you know them well already?

Freddy I know them well. I know that … uh … we drive each other slightly mad [*Yeah.*] but … um …

John It helps to know that.

Freddy Yeah, it's— Uh, it'll be— That'll be fun, I think, three of us. And we all have quite similar lifestyles [*Yes.*] so I think that'll be good 'cos there'll actually be someone around in the evening … uh … to chat to, which is nice.

John Three— three's a good number, I think. Um, I— I've recently moved into a flat with two others and … um … like you say, there's always somebody around but it's never— it never feels crowded. Um, and— and I— I'd never met these people before so— [*Oh, really?*] … um … so yeah, they're— they're both really friendly guys and—… uh … and have similar interests with— with both of them, but sort of different interests as well so—… um … so, again, we don't always have to be in the same place at the same time but— but we can sit down and watch the same TV shows and— and … um … you know, do the same things out of the house as well. And they've become firm friends in just a few months.

Freddy That's good. [*Yeah.*] Yeah, yeah. Well. I always worry about that. [*Yeah.*] I think I— I— I— I can no longer meet new people. Um, I think I've got to— I've become too grumpy. I don't think I could live with someone I hadn't lived with before.

John The trick is to find other grumpy people!

Freddy Ah, right. Is it? Is it?

John That's what I've done. That helps.

Freddy Are you sure?

John Yeah! So we're— all three of us are just grumpy old men together, you see? [*Oh, right.*] It helps.

Freddy Yeah, yeah. Okay. I think— yeah, I think … um … I think that's my worry about moving in with new people is that I— is I'm now fairly intolerant of … uh … [*Of everything.*] people's foibles. So whereas when I've met these guys when I was younger at university and … uh … was— was a really easygoing chap, I—… uh … I've learnt to live with them. Um—

John What— what foibles did they have at university?

Freddy Oh well, you know, these guys— we used to— we were so messy that the bin was— I mean, the bin was never taken out. That was a stand-off situation. Uh, and so we ended up just scraping food onto the kitchen floor and we had, like, maggots in dishes, and … uh … the living room was a sea of chicken bones and Coke cans. Um, and the toilet didn't flush so we used a bucket to flush the water down with. It was actually a beautiful flat. It was one of the nicest flats I've ever seen. [*It sounds it, it really does!*] It was one of the nicest flats I've ever seen, it was just … Uh, yeah, and all that was out of…uh…principle. We're all…uh…sticklers for principle and would…uh…rather live in a complete tip than…uh…be the one to tidy up someone else's mess.

John   Okay. I had the opposite at university. I lived— I lived with a friend…um…who was obsessively clean and tidy and, you know, one of those people who likes to everything at 90 degree angles and…uh…and— and so I didn't really have to do much. He— he did all the cleaning. And if—you know, if a bin bag was— was left full in the corner of the kitchen, he would— he'd be the one to take it out all the— virtually every time. [*Oh, that's good.*] So I didn't really have to worry about that. Um, I— I found out, you know, at the end of— at the end of the year that he had been holding a grudge against me— against me the whole time because he had to do all the work. But, you know, we're still friends so it's okay.

Track 30

Celia   Yeah, and I met Pete at work. Um, yeah, I don't know. I think…um…Yeah, I suppose it was— it was really his sense of humour 'cos he was…um…very sort of charming and funny and…um…yeah. Yeah, and always at the beginning you— you kind of make a real effort. Um, oh, Pete— I— I always pull him up on this – so he wr— he showed me a poem that he'd written when we first started going out. And so this was in the first couple of months, and so I thought he w— he wrote a lot of poetry. He's not— he doesn't! So that was just like the charm offensive. [*Hasn't done it since?*] Yes. So that was quite naughty of him.

Karen   Are you sure he actually wrote it?

Celia   He did – he wrote it, and it rhymed and everything. It was very clever. He's quite creative. I admire that in him. He's very creative and he's very good at music and…um…very musical. Um, he's able to, like, listen— if we're listening to— if we're watching TV and there's a piece of music on the TV…um…he can almost listen and pl— start to play it— [*Wow.*] pretend play— air, you know. He plays the guitar, I think he could probably play the piano, he can play the drums, I think he could play a number of… [*So he's naturally musical.*] Yeah, so amazing. [*That's interesting.*] So yeah. Yeah, he's very creative and I admire that in him 'cause he's just recently gone freelance and…um…my worry was that sometimes I think he's, in business, a little bit too nice – not ruthless enough. But I— on the— on the plus side I think his creativity around marketing himself and marketing— He— For example, he's written— self-published, written a book, and that's really worked for him and really got him in— got his foot in the door in lots of places.

Karen   And that's something that you've found attractive in him?

Celia   Yes, yeah, that's …

Karen   His proactivity [*Yeah.*] and his creativity.

Celia   Yeah. And so what about you and Andy?

Karen   Yeah, it's interesting 'cos I think at the outset of a relationship you think you know the things that are gonna be important to you for compatibility and as you say, a sense of humour is— I think it is important for women. Men like to be laughed at, too, so it's high on their list. Interests— it's nice to have similar interests. Um, but you know, I think with time those things…uh…change. Your interests change, your sense of humour changes [*Mmm.*] and there's got to be other things, I think. An underlying compatibility of values, [*That's true, yes.*] goals. You've got to— Yeah, I think you've basically got to have the same ethical and moral value system, maybe spiritual system. I don't know if that's important to you, but I think that's got to be there as well. And those things generally don't change with time.

Celia   No. [*Um.*] And finance can often— [*Yes, yes. Gosh, yes.*] can make things difficult, just— just whether you have the same kind of— [*Similar approach.*] yeah, approach.

Karen   And are you two quite compatible on money?

Celia   Reasonably compatible, both— we're both quite cautious. But he's more generous than I am and we talk—

Karen   Ah, we're the other way round.

Celia You're more generous than Andy?

Karen Yeah, we're fairly similar but he's much more cautious than me. I would spend and worry later.

Celia Mmm. I suppose another thing, you know, speaking about compatibility— another thing that I have noticed and that has become more important is, you know, whether you're pretty good as a team. [*Yes, definitely.*] Because there's just so many things that you have to do on a daily basis, that— you know—

Karen Just supporting each other [*Exactly.*] and relying on each other.

Karen What else? Driving. We have our biggest rows in the car!

Celia Oh, really?

Karen Navigating! Trying to get from A to B.

Celia So you're navigating or you're driving?

Karen Um, if he's driving— We went on holiday to LA and he did most of the driving cos h— his eyesight's better than mine. I can't see long distances. I couldn't read the road signs. So he did the driving. But then, you know, I was trying to navigate and I couldn't see properly so we ended up sort of swerving all over these eight-lane motorways with the children in the back, having major rows. So we often argue in the car, and the kids just sit and laugh at us now. But … uh …

Celia Maybe— maybe I'm lucky because I— Pete does all the driving. I don't [*Oh, really?*] – I'm not a confident driver.

Karen Oh, I'd much rather drive so I— I tend to—

Celia I imagine if I ever drove, that I would have the worst backseat-driver next to me. He's a very good— he's a very good driver, very confident, he's driven for years. So I— I can just imagine he'd get so annoyed with me cos I would be quite sort of…

Karen Oh Andy's quite good. He's not— he's not too much of a backseat driver, but— I don't know, if he's driving he doesn't seem to feel the need to read any road sign whatsoever. That becomes my job.

Celia Oh, really, as well as driving?

Karen And he's— he's completely incapable of following the sat nav. I don't know whether that's a sort of spatial awareness problem. He can't look at a screen and— and follow it when he's driving. I don't know what that's all about. There's some little gene in there somewhere that's… So that's kind of annoying!

Unit 10   Cultural observations

Track 31

Lauren Um, I think in some ways, it's been easier moving from England than it would have been moving from the United States, certainly, because— partly because, you know, the distance from home is something I've gotten used to by now … um … and partly because there're some rituals in Germany that are more similar to rituals in America than the rituals in England are. For example, in England everyone goes for a Sunday lunch, whereas in both Germany and in the US everyone goes for brunch. Or, you know, in England the bars, or most of the bars, close at 11.30 or 12.30 or later— at latest whereas here, you know, if you go out you may well stay out until one or two in the morning. That isn't wildly different from what you would do in New York, which is where I'd been living before. So some of those little things are actually … um … comforting, in a way that I hadn't necessarily expected.

Dieter I don't— I don't think that we could have done things very much differently. It's always sort of— as it is, we have a— We're— I'm married to an American, she's married to a German, and this cross-cultural … uh … life is just not that easy. It automatically creates … um … problems— organizational problems, first of all. Um, I like the cultural differences, and I— this— uh … You know, I actually enjoy living between two cultures … um … but I don't enjoy all the organizational stuff that goes along with it. Um, but that's just what it is. I think there's not anything that we can make better or that we— stress that we could avoid. I think it just comes with— with this cross-cultural life that we lead.

Lauren Yeah, so a matter of logistical headaches or divorce, and I think we're leaning towards the former at the moment.

Track 32

From my experience th— the family relations in— in the UK … um … in— in many cases are good between the son and the father, … um … the mother and the daughter. But there is no obligation for the person to— to … um … live all the time with his … um … mother and father. Um, it's slightly different in— in Saudi Arabia, where religiously you are encouraged to stay with your … um … parent, especially if they needs— … uh … if they need your help. Then the first option for them is to come over to your house. I'm sure this is in many cases still existing in Britain, but it is not— from what I have seen, it's not the— the norm. Um, there is the … uh … uh … houses for elderlies— … uh … elderly people and— … um … all around the country … uh … which fortunately for Saudi elderly still not— not the case in Saudi Arabia. Although in the recent years there has been some change in the attitudes toward— toward … uh … elderly people but is still— they still within the family in most cases, from my experience.

Uh, also in— in— in Saudi Arabia … um … there is some sort of— Um, within the society there is the— … um … generally, there is a male society and female society. In some cases you can call it segregation but it's not … um … always. Because traditionally the— the tribal … uh … mentality works this way. And … uh … from early days in the Arab history this is— this was the— the case – that there is the woman's section of the house and there is the male— … uh … or … uh … men's section of the house. Uh, usually they— they don't mix. Um, there is some religious reasons for that but … um … some … uh … also justification for this … um … is this is the tradition that we— we— we are brought in, this is the norm. So … um … it's still practised widely in Saudi Arabia. Ev— even in parties that there is the male section of the party … uh … and the female section of the party. The wedding is not mixed. There is the— … um … uh … for example, the— the hall— … um … uh … of— of the— where the groom— where she … um … brought in, will be … uh … hundred percent women. And the … um … groom, will be … uh … with the men in the hall … uh … where all the— a hundred percent of them are men. And the … uh … bride will be among the women and a hundred percent of the people attended in the hall are women. And— and work places and education … uh … and … um … in many … uh … of the hospitals, you will find this separation. So … um …— you would normally … uh … see … uh … and you maybe never see … um … a— a mixed school where … uh … boys and girls … uh … study together. Um, there's no university … um … which provided … uh … mixed education.

And you can imagine for someone … um … uh … like me who— who was brought— brought in this … um … society, and imagine his first day where he encounters his … um … classmates to be … um … female and male students. It wasn't easy, but you have to— to adapt with the situation, given that you will spend five or six years of— of that and you have really to— to— … um … just to work around that, how— how to approach … uh … your— your classmates and speak with them. Um, especially that … uh … to learn English you have to really communicate and … um … speak with— with … uh … your— your colleagues … uh … your mates— your— your classmates, and people everywhere. And if you cannot … um … master this skill, you cannot learn English properly.

Track 33

Advice I would give to any … um … one want to visit Saudi Arabia … uh … and bear in mind that his background or his— … um … he is British, is that … uh … he has to bear in mind that there is different … um … attitudes to different … uh … ideas.

Um, for example, if— if she is a lady, she should expect that there is … um … a— like a code for— for the … um … for the clothing or for the dress. We call this in Saudi Arabia … uh … modesty. Uh, she— which means that she— she has to wear a modest dress. Um … um … it's not, like, revealing anything of— of the— the body. It's not always the case that she has to cover … um … everything the head and the— the hair – but … um … at least … um cover the— the— … um … the body. Um, otherwise she will have some problems with the … um … um … maybe the— from the legal perspective, she will have— she will have … um … a— a— a problem because … um … she might be stopped by— … um … by police and advised to— to wear this … um … we call it *abaya*. So this is something to bear in mind.

Uh, the opposite way, for a lady coming from Saudi Arabia, and if she decides that she— she wants to wear the— the— the traditional ... um ... um ... dress which she usu— usually wears in— in— in Saudi Arabia, she has to bear in mind that the black ... um ... colour is not common ... um ... for women here to wear it, especially if it's covering everything, so she has to bear in mind that. And maybe ... um ... she— ... um ... if she prefer, she— she may go for ... uh ... some of the light colours.

Unit 11   Social media

Track 34

Dan   Yeah, I do have a Twitter account, but I find it difficult to keep up ... um ... with my own life ... uh ... let alone spending lots of time trying to sift through what I ... uh ... what I believe to be relevant information ... um ....

Lily   But wait, isn't the whole point of it that it's meant to be— it's not meant to take up loads of your time?

Dan   I tend— I— I tend to think that the use of websites like Twitter have ... uh ... reduced the level of old-fashioned communication that people have but— it— but at the same time making it easier for people to communicate – just communicate stuff that's of less quality.

Lily   What— yeah, I suppose so. 'Cos people don't have to think as much.

Dan   'Cos people are just talk— people are just talking about how they're gonna go out for a walk and 'OMG, I just saw a really funny dog'.

Lily   But isn't that more Facebook, though? Do people do that on Twitter?

Dan   Yeah, course they do. Twitter is— is just a different— it's the same ... uh ... it's the same type of stuff. Well, like statuses on Tw— on Facebook and Tweets on Twitter are essentially— in my opinion, are essentially the same thing.

Lily   Yeah, but the whole arena's different. Like, you've got an audience on Facebook of people who know you, but if you— if you wrote something controversial on Twitter it could potentially— it goes out to people who— Like, if you were someone with loads of followers, you have to be probably really, really careful about what you say. In fact, that probably makes you think more about what you're writing.

Dan   Sure, but people like you and I, are we gonna have that many followers? Is Brad Pitt gonna care what I say about Angelina Jolie? No.

Lily   Okay, so ... um ... when you're checking on Twitter and stuff, how do you do it? Do you do it on your phone?

Dan   Yeah, mostly on my phone. I don't think I'd ever go on my computer and go on to the Twitter website. That's just a personal preference of mine. It's definitely a mobile thing I think – communicating on the move. That's what— Surely that's one of the main advantages of why it was created? I mean, I'm no expert, but you wouldn't sit down at your computer, turn it on, and then write 150 characters.

Lily   What— How often would you check your phone, then?

Dan   Um, just when I— I— when I have nothing else to do. If I'm— If I'm sitting on a train and— and I've run out of lives on my favourite game, I might go on my Twitter app [*So you basically do it—*] and see what's up. Or actually, if there's something impor— if— if there's something ... uh ... if there's something going on in— in the world that's very important, like breaking news, or in— in football, then I guess I'm drawn more to— to things like Twitter to try and keep up to date. 'Cos Twitter is quite responsive. I dunno. [*If you saw something that was—*] I'd watch the telly, though. I'd switch to the telly, if I had a telly.

Lily   But Twitter's way faster than the telly 'cos you can get a Tweet about something before they've had time to put together a programme about it.

Dan Yeah, true, but— but then— but then it comes down to, like, personal preference and enjoyment. You're not gonna sit in your living room with all the— with the television off and just sit there reading Twitter. [*Yeah, I guess.*] I'd have the telly on, and then maybe do— do some Twitter as well.

Lily And then make sure you're really up to date.

Track 35

David So how often do you use Twitter, Larry?

Larry I don't use Twitter or Facebook.

David Why don't you use them?

Larry Well, with Facebook, it's because I don't really care what other people who I barely know are doing, and I don't really want them – people who barely know me – to get the impression from the few posts that I might do or the hundred posts I might do, that that's who I am. So, I have to confess, I go on my son's Facebook every once in a while to spy on people who I probably haven't seen in twenty years and just wonder what they look like now. But that's the extent of my Facebook. Um, I— I also know myself well enough that if I was gonna get on Facebook or was gonna…um…get on Twitter a lot— I— I might— I do— I do use Twitter sometimes to follow people I find interesting because I like to know what they're thinking or what they're reading, but I also know myself well enough that I'll become obsessed and I'll waste way too much time doing any of those things. Have you?

David I— I think it's interesting. I agree about the wasting time aspect. My personality is— is the same. If I really am interested in something, I will start spending more time on it than I actually should compared to things that I should be spending time on. That said, I— I think I'm in the same boat as you where I don't use my Facebook very often except to catch up and see what people look like and what they're doing. I think the quality of posts on Facebook tends to not be very high. I like to use Twitter more often because I think that on Twitter it's easier to be selective of who you wanna follow and it's therefore easier to have a Twitter account that is only filled with things that you think are relatively intelligent, as opposed to seeing what my friend from high school who I haven't spoken with in ten years had for breakfast this morning.

Larry I— I just read a survey – I can't remember where it was, but it was in the last few weeks – saying that most people now find social media an obligation rather than fun. And I think that's— once it crosses that line, then I think people drop out.

David I think a great example of that is— is LinkedIn. But I use LinkedIn a lot to see what other people are doing and what jobs change and if people post interesting information. But I think LinkedIn is the first social network that people don't use for fun. They use it because you feel like if you're not in LinkedIn then you're gonna be missing out on something, and that you might not know about a great job that you wanna go after, or you might not know that one of your friends has moved from one company to another. And I think that Twitter is getting into that same space. And I think a lot of people who work in media, publishing, communications, do feel that obligation that 'if I'm not on Twitter, I'm at a disadvantage to everyone that I'm around who has an easier way of considering this constant array of news'. And so, like anything that becomes an obligation instead of a fun activity, it is gonna die. Die might be a strong word but it's going to lose its, kind of, spontaneous appeal.

Track 36

Rachael It's— you know on Facebook you have a picture— of a pro— a profile picture, [*Yeah, yeah, yeah.*] whether it's you [*Yeah. Yeah.*] and— and maybe a little short description of yourself? Well, that's the same as Twitter. So you could go on my profile   you could— I've got a picture of me [*Okay.*] and I'm actually called rachworld. [*Aww, okay.*] Right. And I don't have anything about myself – I just say I'm actually from the Lake District. [*Okay.*]

Alison A lot of these people just sort of— It's really boring, mundane stuff, like…um…'oh, I'm having Cheerios for breakfast this morning' and that sort of thing. I mean, who wants to know all that?

Rachael	I think— I— some people probably do that, not— I think maybe on Facebook a lot of people do such—stuff like that.
Alison	Do they, on Facebook too?
Rachael	I call— and I— I call a lot of the stuff on Facebook 'humble bragging'.
Alison	Well, I think it's all bragging!
Rachael	'Let's— let's make my life sound better.' But on Twitter, I think it's short and sweet. And I don't find that as much because I mainly follow well-known people, [*Okay.*] not particularly friends.
Alison	But are you— Is your phone not always buzzing? Do you not find it really takes over? Like, you— you— your phone must be constantly— You know, if everybody's constantly Tweeting and Retweeting and everything else, surely you're— your phone's forever buzzing and it's—
Rachael	I don't get that many Retweets, to be fair. [*Oh!*] I— To be fair, I only Tweet— Most of my posts are that I will probably Retweet somebody else— what somebody else has said that I think is a great Tweet. [*Okay.*] And I'll say 'oh I'll let my friends'— my followers, sorry, not my friends— 'my followers see it.' And at the minute I have— I did have thirty followers, I've now only got twenty-eight. [*Aww.*]

Unit 12   Attitudes to work

Track 37

Karen	I've lived in Hong Kong, I've lived in Sweden, I've lived in Singapore. Um, when I lived in Sweden I was single, I was teaching. So you just tended to do the hours you needed to do and go home and that was fine. And I think as a society they had a pretty good balance of work and leisure.
Celia	In Sweden?
Karen	Yes. [*Mmm.*] Yeah.
Celia	So I heard— 'Cos … um … I used to work for a Swedish company, and so I went to Stockholm in the winter, and they— they told me that they— their particular company, they had shorter hours in the summer [*Yes, yes.*] and longer in the winter so you could enjoy the— [*maximize the light, yeah.*] yeah. That's a really good idea, I think.
Karen	Yeah, yes it is. Yes, they were quite flexible that way. Um, when I was living in Hong Kong first time, yeah, I was single then, too. Oh gosh yes, that was a work hard, play hard situation. I was teaching, I worked six days a week um … I think I finished at about five on a Saturday and then we'd generally go out and party til probably 3am! Sleep half of Sunday and then start work again at 8 o'clock Monday morning. [*Wow.*] So it was— it was tough. But, you know, I was young, twenty-three or something, and that's what you do when you're that age. Um, the time we lived in Singapore, I had— well, I had one child when we arrived, I had a second child while I was there and the problem there was that I was in a travelling job, so I was away a lot [*Mmm.*] Um, for up to a week at a time.
Celia	That was tough?
Karen	Travelling— covering Asia, mostly. Um, but my husband's a teacher so he does— he, at the time, did relatively short hours. He doesn't now, actually – he works very long hours. But he used to do fairly short hours at the international school, and he was the primary carer with the children. We had also a— a lady who lived with us in the house … um … who was fabulous and just like one of the family. [*Mmm.*] So she helped and … um … and we employed a nanny who had the children – well, had the baby anyway – from 8am til 3 every day. So we had a good support system around us that enabled me to do the hours I needed to do in my job [*Mmm.*] but I still tried to be home— when I wasn't travelling I tried to be home by— well, in time for bath time. So I would try to be home by 6.30 [*Mmm.*] so I could at least do the evening routine – bath time and a story and all that kind of thing. And I didn't have to start work before 8.30 and it was a fairly short commute

so it wasn't actually too bad when I was there. [*Mmm.*] Um, but the travel was a problem and I became pretty … um … disillusioned with it by the end [*Mmm.*] and just wanted to be at home.

Celia   It's exhausting, travelling, isn't it? [*Yeah, yeah. It was.*] It sounds real— really glamorous and I think for a short—

Karen   Yeah, no, it's not really.

Celia   For a short time [*Yeah.*] it can be, but then after a while it's quite wearing.

Karen   Yeah, and if you're doing it for a whole week and then you're back for a week and then you're away again for another week—

Celia   It's quite unsettling, isn't it?

Karen   To do that for two or three years is— when you've got a young family as well—

Celia   That's really tough, yeah.

Karen   I mean, I really— when Madeleine was two and a half I— I didn't really feel I knew her. [*Mmm.*] I'd come home from trips and she'd gone through a whole development stage and [*Mmm.*] I'd missed it, so that wasn't great, really. Um, fortunately she doesn't remember it now so … Um, so yeah, that was tough.

Track 38

I think working in Austria is quite different to working in the UK. Um, I've done both. So when I started my career, I … uh … started off … uh … working in Austria … um … in an office … uh … where we produced – manufactured – computers, basically. And … um … so basically the main difference, I found, is— I mean, the office where I worked in Austria was literally my hometown, so my commute was … um … walkable … um … cyclable, and it was literally just, like, five minutes down the road. Um, so in the end it made the day a lot longer … um … because, you know … um … you just finished work … um … at five or something and then you were back home at ten past five or you meet— you— you were meeting friends … um … in the city centre. It's not— you don't have to plan as much. Now I work in London and … um … you know, my commute is about an hour cycling or forty-five minutes … um … with— on the tube. And that actually takes two hours off— off your day … um … apart fr— You know, you're getting out of the office and it takes you another hour to get back home. So the day's a lot shorter and the evenings are a lot shorter as well.

However, what I really like about working in the UK is that everything starts later. So … um … we're starting to work at, like, nine, quarter past nine, half past nine … um … whereas in Austria you gotta be there by eight o'clock, so you gotta get up at, like, seven or something like that. If you want to do some sports before work, you're getting up at six. And that's not unusual – like, people just do that. But I constantly found myself being horribly tired so— Um, I guess in terms of work/life balance there is advantages and disadvantages everywhere. If you're an early riser, Austria or Germany are your countries because you can do your work in the morning and then you're getting out of the office a bit earlier. You don't have that much of a commute as well.

Um, so the attitude … um … is also quite different. The attitude towards work in Austria is really— I— I— I think Austria's a funny in-between … Um, you know, it's in between … um … the Italian, you know, 'we really work to live' … um … attitude and the German, you know, we— we—we— you know, 'our life is all about work' attitude. So in Austria you have a kind of funny mix about both but I— I do think that people … um … kind of try and … um… work so they have a little bit of money and try and get more out of their lives and have a very active social lives and family life. Family's very important. Whereas … um … working in London … um … I think … um … all about your identity and all about your— your— your life— you identify yourself with what you do and what you do as a job is very important … um … for your life …

Unit 13   Charities

Track 39

My dad…um…he was diagnosed with cancer, and it— it all happened very quickly. Um, he was diagnosed in July and he died in November. And it was a very tough time. And going through that— And also he— he was only 65— just 65 when he died. And that made me put things into perspective and I thought I really need to do something I really want to do, because life is short and if I want do something I have to do it now.

So it was a— it was a very difficult decision because I…um…obviously, I had a mortgage and I…uh…I need to pay my mortgage. And it— it was tough because obviously…um…I had decided by then that I wanted to work for a cancer charity and it was going to be very difficult to— to make that sort of change. So I spoke to some people who had done it and…um…I thought it's now or never. So I resigned from my job. Um, and so I left my job in August and I think people thought…um…that I was mad because I left with nothing at all. And I decided to take a couple of weeks off, doing nothing, watching telly at home, and then I got bored. And I thought 'I'm going to— to volunteer'.

So…um…Macmillan, who's a cancer charity…uh…they had opportunities for— for volunteering, so I got in touch with them and they found me something to do. It was— it was very basic…uh…but I enjoyed it and I was with—…um…with them for about a— a month or it was actually two months, doing something quite routine but I really, really enjoyed it and— even doing something that was quite boring…um…gave me satisfaction because I knew where the money was going on and so. Um, I met the people there and I— I really enjoyed the organization and there was—um…they advertized…um…a role that I thought I could do and I applied. I didn't get it. And then I continued applying and then a— a couple of weeks later was another one and I got that one. And I've been there for, I don't know, since then, so two and a half years or something. Um, I'm very happy and I've— I've made progress so now I manage my own team and I love it. So…um…I would say to people who are not sure about what to do in—…um…with their career, that just go for it, if— if you can afford it. And not to be scared. And if you really show that you want to do it…um…I think you— you can change careers from something quite different. And the— the experience that I got from working in a corporate environment has helped me…um…quite a lot because…um…I've got skills that, you know, they appreciate.

We do lots of things. I mean, people know us because we've got nurses that go around to people and also they are based in hospitals, and they help people with cancer. But we also give…um…grants to— to people who need money and…um…for example…um…one of the…uh…lovely stories…um…I've heard of…um…I was on the phone, because I used to be on the phone talking to supporters and taking donations and sometimes people tell you their stories. And there was this lady who…um…had been diagnosed with cancer and…um…we gave her a small amount of money to go and visit her son in the other end of the country, spend a couple of days with him, have a break, and tell him in person that she had been diagnosed. And we managed to do that. Um, there was another…um…story of this…um…uh…father who had small children and it was October and he was not going to make it till Christmas, and we paid for the children to have a Christmas party with him. Uh, and we also pay for wedding dresses…uh…washing machines, anything. So that's something we do. We've got a support line, people can phone us…uh…just talk to us and they may feel a bit better. We can give them advice. Um, we help people with benefits. So for example, can they get some money from the government, get some help? So it's quite…um…varied, but the— the stories are very touching…uh…and they are not all sad stories. We've got very…um…positive stories of people who— who get cured and they phone us. And I remember another call that really touched me – somebody phoned and said 'I want to make a donation today because I got the all-clear, and you helped me and I just want to say thank you'. So we— we get all sorts of stories, and they are all very touching. Um, so that's— that's what we do.

Track 40

Denis   My favourite charities are probably ones that are health-related – cancer charities probably, because I believe that all of us— all of us at some point will have been touched by someone that has suffered cancer.

Sally   So has that— has that come out of a personal experience that you would choose that?

Denis   I lost— I lost my own father through cancer. I know that he was— a lot of the treatment he had was really only found, if you like, through a lot of charitable funding.

Sally   Yeah, okay. 'Cos I work for the Stroke Association, as I think you know, and one of the things that's always really surprised me is that stroke affects such a massive number of the population but it's way behind charitable giving for cancer and heart, so I'm inclined to now think I'm not gonna give money to cancer 'cos so many people do, and I'd rather give money to smaller charities that just don't get the amount of money because cancer and heart conditions seem to be sort of like glamorous-type – you can have good outcomes.

Denis   But because a lot of people do suffer strokes, if everyone that has been touched by that gave to the appropriate charity, it would be a lot more equal, wouldn't it?

Sally   It would, but I think people don't. And I think it's because people see stroke as an old person's condition, whereas some charities, like cancer and heart and so on…um…and children's charities, are ones that have the real sort of 'ah!' factor or have…um…good outcomes like you can— the— the research can be used to show that you can…um…operate or treat heart and the cancer and everything'll be okay, whereas some charities…um…are working to just improve the quality of life for people and I think sometimes that's not seen as 'sexy' charity.

Denis   Perhaps they just need more publicity.

Sally   But do you feel, though, that if— if you— you say that you would readily give to cancer charities – if— if you knew that cancer is one of the…um…charities that is given to most of all, that's got lots of money, would that make you feel differently about what you gave money to?

Denis   But I will also give to heart charities and— and the stroke charities.

Sally   You would, so—

Denis   Yeah, yeah, I don't have a problem with that. Human— human charities I be— I believe in, [*Okay, but*—] much— much more higher up than a lot of animal charities.

Sally   Yeah, yeah, I agree with you, yeah. I do. 'Cos I sometimes feel a bit bad that I walk past things in supermarkets, you know when they have those boxes out and they say 'put food in' and stuff for…um…animals, like PDSA, and people put food and things. [*Tins of cat food and things.*] Sometimes it really sort of makes me feel quite bad that I just walk past them. But if I've got money I feel I could direct into charity that wouldn't be my first priority.

Denis   I— I don't think it should make you feel bad walking past them. I mean, y— people can only give a certain amount. You can't give to everything.

Sally   But don't you feel bad when you get all those envelopes through the door that—?

Denis   No, I just throw them in the bin. I still give t— I still give to charities I want to give to. But what I don't like are charities that bombard you on your way out of a supermarket [*Yeah*] because they think you've got your purse in your pocket, or your wallet in your pocket.

Sally   The ones I really hate are the ones that try to sign you up for something and then give you all the sob stories and then— but actually they don't want a pound there and then – they want you to sign up for regular giving. And that makes me feel really bad.

Denis   Yeah, for the rest of your life.

Sally   Well, hopefully not that long! Probably forget about it half an hour later. But some of those letters and things that you get through the post tell really worthwhile stories. And that's what I mean about the cancer charity bit, really, is that if you've only got, say, a limited income that you can give to charity every year, sometimes I think, 'well, if I know that cancer and heart charities are getting loads of money coming in anyway, should I ignore those to give it to the smaller, just as worthwhile, charities?

Unit 14   Collecting

Track 41

I think … uh … whatever you want to collect – whether it's silver or … uh … small bits of furniture or— or tea caddies or art or paintings, you've got to have a passion for it. You've got to really enjoy it and appreciate it. So you look at an object, or you look at an item, and you think 'I really like that'. And … um … you can find examples on the Internet. A lot of people now— there are various websites that you can … um … look at and you'll see— lots of antique dealers will advertize on them as well, lots of auction houses. Um, and there are a number of these sites that you can look at. And once you know what you want to collect and what you're looking for, then you can specialize in certain areas and certain websites, and that's a good way of finding … um … a— particular objects. Also … um … auctions – you can tour round the auctions, which I find great fun, really – trying to find … uh … nice objects. And you can go to antique fairs – there are lots and lots of antique fairs all over the world, … um … some, sort of, very cheap … uh … antique fairs, sort of almost like a car boot sale, and the other end of the scale, beautifully stand-fitted and, you know, very exuberant-looking antique fairs. So … um … you can look at antique fairs. And … um … antique shops. Um, just go down your high street, or— or wherever you are. Um, and— and antique centres – there are lots of antique centres around … um … which will house a whole mixture … um … of things – ev— any sort of antique, whether it's silver or furniture or paintings or art or … So there's several places to go to find your— your treasures, whatever you want to start collecting. But the important thing is— I think, is to— is to have a passion about it, is to be— is to be passionate about whatever you want to collect, and always try to get the very best.

Track 42

Uh, it kinda started when I got a book about birds and I started to really be interested in birds. I started to collect those cards with lots of different types of birds. But what's quite weird with me is I tend to collect stuff and then stop and don't bother about it anymore. So I did this … um … and then when I got my first … uh … camera, we went to the *Châteaux de Loire* quite often because I— I'm actually not really far away from there and … uh … I started to be obsessed with Renaissance architecture, to the point where I was— every time we were going to a castle I would, like, really … uh … force my parents to buy me all the postcards they could on each castle and then I would compile them in books – like, ordering them by castle and very complex thing. Plus I would then add also the pictures I had taken so it was a very elaborate albums, taking notes of what I was seeing.

So, like, that's something I did for quite a long time and then the castle kinda went quiet … uh … as I hit … uh … teenagehood, and I started to be … um … obsessed with films. So I started to collect posters of films and I would have to put them, like, pretty much like any teenagers – I would, like, collect them and put them in my room one by one by one by one, like that. Things like that.

I also … um … at some point collected stamps and I had, like, about five or six books full of stamps from lots of different places. And that's something that came from my old aunt that used to give me lots of stuff. So we were, like, meeting up and she would tell me about the stamps and we'd share and exchange stuff about the collections.

Again, stamps kind of went out of fashion quite quickly and … uh … when I was a teenager, the big one that I did was collecting all my trainers that I used to buy. I think I started when I was thirteen. And I started to keep them, basically. So Adidas, Nike, Reebok … um … Vans – all the kind of, like, different stages of my life where I was more a skater person, more like … um … someone who liked wearing the … um … Stan Smith or more, like, Converse, all different colours of Converse. And I'm still doing it now – I still have lots of shoes and my girlfriend is a bit complaining about it every now and then, but that's alright.

And what's quite interesting is collecting actually became— became my job because I started to work in the museum sector and I worked at the Science Museum for a while. And I ended up there collecting mobile phones – that was just something that happened on a project. So I started to catalogue and obsessively read about the types of mobile phones one should have if you wanted to have quite a collections of mobile phones. I also met lots of people who were collecting mobile phones, not as a hobby but almost as a job, to the point where I, for example, wanted to collect stuff from Japan so I found someone actually had lots of Japanese mobile phones, and kinda exchanging stuff about it. Or also phones in Africa because they're different, so I actually organized a project where I would go to Cameroon to collect the phones and bring them back to the UK so that they went to the collection at the museum. So I'm a bit of a collecting freak, even though my collections are sometimes quite randomly chosen.

Track 43

I got started collecting fountain pens probably when I was maybe twenty. Um, my handwriting was always very, very poor and I thought if I had a fountain pen, I could … uh … write more beautifully and that my writing would be easier to read, or more legible. I started off relatively simply … um … with a relatively inexpensive fountain pen – it wasn't a collection. But one purchase led to another and another and I started to develop fountain pen envy. Um, I would see other people with particularly attractive fountain pens. Once I took a trip to Paris, for example … um … and I saw a beautiful pen there and I just really, really was intrigued … um … by that pen and wanted to have one. So I saved up my money … um … and I— and I got that pen. Um, and all along the way, I started … um … gathering more and more fountain pens. I didn't intend it to be a collection, but after five and six and seven pens, it started to look like one. At about that time my handwriting was really good … um … because I'd invested in these pens, I also was taking more— paying more attention to my writing in the process.

Um, and then I realized I could acquire vintage fountain pens. Those are antique fountain pens that were made in the 1920s or the 1930s … um … and I was really interested in the fact that these pens still worked … um … eighty, ninety years later. So I became very interested in vintage fountain pens in particular. Um, there's an American brand called … uh … Parker, and also a German company called Pelican who made beautiful … um … pens … um … in that period. And so increasingly I started to look for vintage fountain pens, and that was really interesting to collect because instead of just going into a shop, you could find … um … them in a— in a flea market … um … or online from … uh … someone who had collected them themselves, and there were lots of different outlets where I could … um … buy my vintage fountain pens.

So that— that's pretty much … um … the extent of my collection. I think I probably have about thirty to forty pens now. Um, when people come to my house I don't display them in a glass case or anything … um … I'm a little more disorganized than that, so— but I know where they all are and I get them out … um … if people want to see them. Um, I have one— I think my prized possession— there's a Japanese pen that I have … um … that has really exquisite … uh … details on it. Um, it's a very beautiful pen and I even had the nib … uh … ground down at an angle to replicate the kind of nibs — which is the very end of the pen – … um … the kind of nibs that people used to use in the forties and fifties. So again, a very vintage feel.

Unit 15   Music

Track 44

Wang   And as for traditional Chinese music, I prefer some … uh … Chinese classical music. Um, I think they are really … um … just like the Western classical music … uh … they are very famous and I think they sound very soothing. I like listen to them sometimes when I'm alone.

Zhang   Can you name some?

Wang   Um, I can name a— In Chinese, it's *'Chun Jiang Hua Yue Ye'* and maybe can translate into … uh … 'spring river on a moonlight night'. I don't know how to translate. But I like it very much.

Zhang   Yes I—… um … me too. I haven't listened to that since, like, ten years ago.

Wang   Oh yeah. Because they are classics, they will last forever.

Zhang   Yes. But also I notice that in— in China now, that many … uh … rock stars, since rock's not that popular in China, but the rock stars also have some— they— they put some traditional Chinese elements in their music. So probably they use some instruments or they use— they sing opera or something else during the performance. [I—] You know someone like that? They have   I think the … um … Tang Dynasty band, when they—

Wang   Tang Dynasty?

Zhang   They— they are— they are old now. There's no— th— that band was dismissed…uh…like, five years ago. Um, but they used to have a very popular song called 'Back to Tang Dynasty in a Dream' and they sing quite classic Chinese…um…kind of opera but also rock mixture and it's a— it's a huge popular— it was huge popular among— at that time. Uh, maybe ten, fifteen years ago, among college students.

Wang   I think I'm too young at that time so I never heard this rock band before.

Zhang   Yeah. Rock's never— never been…um…mainstream [*Yeah.*] in China anyway.

Track 45

Krishna   Cinema in India's a big passion. Um, and…uh…Bollywood…uh…being the largest. Uh, we— we also have…uh…regional level actors – every state has got their own big stars…um…acting in movies, but Bollywood is, like, a pan-India thing. And they are very big stars. Um, and…uh…this year I think Bollywood is celebrating hundred years— [*Yeah.*] hundred years of cinema in India. And it's a huge passion, it's a huge dream for a lot of people – a lot of middle-class people. People go to Bombay, try and…uh…try and get hauled into movies if they can, so they're— it's a big aspirational thing for a lot of Indians.

Neeraj   Yeah, and it has actually evolved over the years, because, you know, what we've seen in the past…uh…uh… there used to be a lot of movies that would be either musicals or based on hist—…uh…historical events but…uh…now we've started addressing issues of today. A lot of movies are theme-based, a lot of movies are based on…uh…major events, sports – so we're trying to cover all that now. And…um…in terms of presentation also we have seen a lot of improvement – …um…a lot of special effects…uh…which…uh…we are trying to replicate from what happens in Hollywood. And, you know, the s— the standards are really getting better there. And, of course, talking about actors…uh…there are so many, and, you know, every month we have, like, more and more being added. But the stars are, like, you know, there are so many and they have huge fan fo— following and…uh…not only in India but all across the world. There are some actors who are, like, …um…uh… I wouldn't say all across India but, like, how— what my colleague just now mentioned, that there are some regional actors. And…uh…from whichever regions they come, they are so big that they are actually worshipped there – they have temples…uh…in their names! So th – that's how it works.

Krishna   I think the best part for me is…uh…the songs and dances in the movies. It's—…um…compared to Hollywood, you don't get to see all that stuff. And…uh…some of the songs…uh…become big hits…uh…after the movie is released or even before the movie is out. So these are very fun things – …uh…people watch them all the time in India on television. They go to a movie, they go— when they go to watch movies then they're— they're crazy about some of the songs, so… And — But yes, it's a— it's a big thing…uh…for the— for the students, especially the younger age group. Uh, they tend to go out and watch a movie after the college or— or…uh…during the weekends, it's a big…uh…pastime for them. They spend at least—…uh…couple of movies every weekend they watch. And I've had friends…uh…I haven't seen them…uh…like, every weekend they go and watch a movie, or at least…uh…couple of them. Plus they watch on the television. So Bo— Bollywood is really big, it's all over— in the newspapers, out on the television. So— and they are big stars, as Neeraj said.

Neeraj   Yeah, and also what Krishna is mentioning about…uh…music – earlier it would be like, you know, a lot of people would talk about running around trees when it comes to Indian songs but things have changed there also. We have some really good music coming out now. And…uh…music earlier in India used to be only film music…uh…but…uh…be it because of Western influence or be it because of…uh…H—…uh…Bollywood movies…uh…there is a lot of…uh…evolution that has happened around music also in India. We have, like, rock bands also. Of course, the music is being used in Bollywood but…uh…they do a lot of shows and they—…uh…they also have a good amount of fan following.

Krishna And this— this— the Bollywood movies … uh … are released all over the world simultaneously, and they have big captive audience, outside India as well when it comes to US or the UK, and even in other parts of the world … uh … like the Middle East. So it is not just India which … uh … the producer is focusing on – it's kind of a global phenomenon now. And they sell rights to a lot of companies before they release the movie so it's— it's really big … uh … business …

Unit 16   Environment

Track 46

My name's Nick Hill. I work in the marine and freshwater … um … international team at the Zoological Society of London. Um, ZSL is an international conservation charity … um … working in fifty countries worldwide, and one of the projects we work on and— and one of the places we've done a lot of work is in the Philippines … um … where we run a project called Net-Works. Um, Net-Works is a really exciting initiative … um … very different and a— a lot of fun for us to all work on. Um, and the objective of Net-Works is to … um … turn old, discarded fishing nets … um … in the— in the central Philippines eventually into carpet tiles, which I put on the floors of people's houses and offices in different parts of the world.

Um, so discarded fishing nets are made from nylon, which is a form of plastic … um … that is very high-grade … um … plastic. Um, so it's an engineering plastic and it has a lot of uses – it's quite valuable. Um, it's al— it's used in fishing nets, particularly, in its purest form, and also in carpets in— in its purest form. But it's also used in computers … um … car tyres, all sorts of different things. Um, when it's used in fishing nets … um … then those fishing nets are often monofilament fishing nets … um … which means that they are— they catch on things very easily … um … so they catch the fish very easily. Um, but the trouble is they get damaged after a bit of time, and after two or three months these nets are damaged and ripped and they don't catch fish as well as they used to. So at this point the fishermen often throw the nets away. In places like the central Philippines … um … which are— in rural, remote communities … um … very poor communities, they don't have access to the same sort of recycling and waste management services that we do … um … in the UK. Um, so most of the time people just throw them on the beach or just dump them in the sea, which is a real problem for the environment. The plastic can last for up to six hundred years before it degrades … um … and then during that time if it's in the sea or on the beaches then it can continue to catch and ensnare marine life, which is a process called ghost-fishing. So it's called ghost-fishing because these— these nets catch … um … the fish and the fish die, the crabs die, and they rot … um … but they don't actually have any benefit for any of the people. So it's reducing the fish catches of the local people and really having a negative impact on their income.

Now this is very bad in these contexts as well, especially in the Philippines because … um … fish catches … uh … have been decreasing for a long time … um … so people's income have been decreasing for a long time. Now, many of these places are heavily, heavily over-fished, so any additional pressure such as g—… um … ghost-fishing is really not very helpful. So it doesn't just affect— have a terrible effect on the environment and the marine life and its—… um … that … um … lives there, … um … it also has a very negative effect on the local communities and populations that live there and depend upon that marine life. The fishers in the central Philippines that we work with are— are completely dependent on the sea one way or another— they … um … mostly for fishing but also for— they do some seaweed farming and other activities in the sea. Um, so yeah, this has a serious cons—… um … negative consequence for them.

Um, and the thing that really makes our project different is that we— we have set up community-based supply chains … um … to be able to collect nets off the beaches and out of the environment, and also to get nets from the fishers after they have finished using them so that they don't throw them into the sea. Um, so the fishers can sell their nets to community groups that we set up, and then the community groups aggregate all of those nets, make sure they're clean and ti— and nice. And then they sell them to us as one group … um … and we— we sell them on to— we send— take—… um … help— help them or facilitate them reach that— reach a market. Um, and those nets actually got to Slo— Slovenia, where there's the only recycling plant in the world … um … for nylon. So that's not something that they can easily sell— send their nets to directly without our help. So we set up these kind of community groups … um … who— who can do the buying within the communities …

Track 47

In Korea...um...they have—...um...these days they— they have more and more...um...effort they— they— they make...um...to keep the environment clean. For example...um...maybe the most commonplace environmental effort they make is...uh...recycling. They have— there is three system of recycling – so every household needs to divide their waste by category. And I think there are, like, four or five different categories there. So maybe we need to put...um...plastic and paper and glass materials and also sometimes batteries. We— we need to everything by categories there. So for example, I live in a big apartment complex and there is a big collection point and if you go there you can see five or six different containers there and every container has a name tag there, which says dead batteries and plastics and vinyl and paper. So we need to take out our garbage and then divide everything by category and put them nicely in the designated container. Otherwise, sometimes the security guards and then the handyman comes along and they give us a warning, or sometimes you can be fined for that.

Another thing is there is a very big thing going on about food waste. Usually Korean food has a lot of liquid there so they do things on weight and also the smell has been a big issue. So the Korean government...um...enforced an act that forces all the residents in apartment complexes to process the...uh...food waste in a designated machine. So if we put food waste there, that— the— the— the machine actually weighs the food waste and then they give you every day target for that. So every month, by the weight of the food waste we throw away, we need to pay. So because we need to pay, everyone in Korea tries to reduce the— the amount of— of food waste every day. I think this method...um...has been making a drastic change in terms of food waste.

And...um...in addition to this kind of...uh...everyday household effort, there is also...uh...a big campaign going on about the reduction of the CO_2. So there is a school assignment about CO_2 reduction. So every summer elementary school gives an assignment about measuring the amount of CO_2 every household consumes. So the children, they need to...uh...watch how much CO_2 every household produces. So because of this...um...raising awareness assignment...uh...everyone should be aware of how much CO_2 we produce. So that way I think we can actually reduce the amount of CO_2 we produces every day.

Unit 17   Weddings

Track 48

Krishna In India, weddings are a big thing. Um, it's— it's like a carnival. Uh, people— lots of people come over— attend the wedding. Uh, you have all your relations, sisters, brothers, cousins, uncles, aunts are coming and staying with the family for a couple of days at least because the wedding takes such a long time. And generally for— I think even now...uh...most of the weddings are arranged. Uh, like...uh...the bride and groom's father— parents...uh...meet and—...um...and the boy and see— they arrange for the marriage. Um, the boy gets to see the girl, they talk to each other. They will not know each other before the wedding but...uh...that's how it happens mostly. But things are changing in India at the moment so people tend to fall in love and get married...uh...but still the majority of the weddings are arranged...uh...in India.

Neeraj Yeah, yeah. And then the kind of ceremonies would also be different...uh...depending on the region but...uh...usually it's— it's never a one-day affair, like how Krishna said – it can go on for several days. And...uh...you know, I mean— and all this while, all the relatives and all the friends should be there at your home. And—...uh...you know, and there's always celebrations happening, a lot of music and dance and—...uh...you know, and some meals being organized and it's, like, a very big affair. And even before the wedding actually happens...uh...how they prepare for the wedding and the amount that is spent on jewellery and clothes – it's, like, a lot.

Krishna And...um...the wedding in each— Uh, India is a big country so the wedding in each region, each state, is a different kind of an affair. Um, like, I am from South India so the weddings...uh...in South India— in Bangla – I'm basically from Bangla – are completely different to what— what it is in north, like Delhi or Punjab or any other state. Um, the costumes are different, the culture is different...um...the ceremony is different, the amount of time it takes...uh...the ceremonies...uh...that's completely different from what is— what we see in North India or East or West. So there's a huge cultural difference ... uh ... in each of the weddings. And ... um ... like ... uh ... at my wedding there were at least ... uh ... seven, eight hundred people, if not less— less than that. So it was a huge affair with so many people attending the ceremony. Then ... uh ... you— you have to host a lunch or dinner depending on the time of the wedding. So, in— at my wedding—... uh ... it happened in the morning ... uh ... so we hosted a lunch for such a big crowd. And the lunch is—... uh ... lunch in South India's completely different again from what ... uh ... you get in north. Uh, so the South Indians generally have a lunch on a plantain leaf, which is spread out well. And there's so many varieties of foods ... uh ... which includes ... uh ... desserts and a lot of sweet dishes. Uh, so it's— it's a very lavish thing ... uh ... a lot of money being spent. And ultimately, the— the people who come and attend the wedding, they— they bless the couple and also gift ... uh ... something from their side. So that's how the weddings are. Uh ...

Neeraj And one thing I've noticed of late is some of the wedding I've attended, the dance—... uh ... some of the dance functions they have is usually a day or two before the wedding. Uh, and these events, they have taken it to a level where, you know, they call in choreo— choreographers ... uh ... and they give special training to people who— who— who have to dance during this—... uh ... this ceremony. And a lot of effort is being put there also.

Krishna And the rich families ... uh ... spend a lot of money, they're— they're very lavish. Uh, sometimes they do tend to waste lot of money, the kind of wastage ... uh ... in terms of food and ... um ... other things ... uh ... which is not a good thing actually – there are so many poor people living in India. So thinking—... uh ... considering all that, a lot of money is being wasted. Um, and the rich families go to any extent. Uh, the— they have their weddings—... uh ... children's weddings at the five star hotels, blow up a lot of money, very expensive gifts are being exchanged. So it happens at all scales, at all levels. Uh, you— you find a poor family which— which is a very small affair. Uh, it goes up to— up to very lavish weddings in India.

Neeraj Yeah, and people— Uh, no matter if you're rich or poor, you end up spending ... uh ... more money than you can actually afford to do on your wedding in India!

Track 49

Lorna So, tell me, how are the wedding plans going?

Nikki They're fine, they're fine. It's only three weeks to go, which is a little bit scary.

Lorna Oh, you must be so excited.

Nikki I am but I'm— I'm quite nervous as well. But yeah, no, I am excited, I really am. I just— I just— I can't wait for it to happen now. We've been planning it for— well, for six months – so yeah, I can't wait. I had a— I had a long phone call with my mother-in-law-to-be last night, [Oh.] and, so you know Patrick's American? And, um, it's just weird – like– we're having the wedding in Scotland, you know, and so it's mostly a Scottish wedding but then because he's American there are little things that are gonna happen I think that are, it— it— it's— it has more of an American flavour than I thought it would.

Lorna Oh right.

Nikki And some of it I think is ... um ... stuff that I expected and some of it I— just things that I had no idea were differences between American and British weddings. Like ... um ... oh, let me think of an example. Like, the rehearsal dinner, for example – we don't really have rehearsal dinners in Britain...

Lorna I've never been to one.

Nikki No, no. And they're a massive thing in America. Like— so she was asking me last night, 'So, what about the rehearsal dinner? When's that happening?' and I was like, 'Mmm, yeah, we're not having one of those.'

Lorna Crikey.

Nikki Yeah. And—

Lorna Wh— what does that actually involve, a rehearsal dinner? Wh— why do you need to have one?

Nikki Well, I think it's … um … it is literally so that they can— well, partially, I think it— it's so they can walk through the ceremony and do the whole ceremony with everybody in their right places and things, so that everybody knows what they're gonna be doing. It always happens the night before the wedding. And— it— But I think the other reason now is that it just— it gets all of the bridal party together and gives them another reason to kind of spend some time together and— because they're the most important people, or they're supposed to be the most important part … um … part, the most important part of the day and of the guest list. But for me, I want it to be all about the day, and not the night before, so I'm not really keen to run through everything the night before.

Lorna I suppose it might help … um … anybody with cold feet. I'm sure [*Yeah.*] you're both really excited about the day but as— just kind of nerves going up to it – if you've had a kind of easy-going run-through beforehand, [*Yeah.*] it might be quite helpful.

Nikki Um, and the other thing that I'm really nervous about— about the American part, is that in America, when you … um … when you have your wedding cake, you have to feed— the bride and groom feed each other a piece of wedding cake.

Lorna Oh.

Nikki I know, and that's a bit weird, but I— that's fine, that's part of their, you know, their— their custom and that's fine, but in some weddings, the groom stuffs the cake into the bride's face. And I'm so scared that Patrick might do that! And I— so I had to warn him the other night that that is not acceptable, he's not allowed to stuff the cake into my face. But I don't really know how common it is, because I'm not American, I've never been to an American wedding. I just read about it.

Lorna And you've not told me what I think is the most important part: is Patrick going to wear a kilt?

Nikki He is! He is gonna wear a kilt, yeah. Obviously in America they wouldn't wear kilts … um … in America they would wear a— a suit, but his— he doesn't really like suits very much and I think he associates them with work … um … so he was really keen to wear a kilt, actually, [*Fantastic.*] which I'm delighted about, yeah.

Lorna And what about your family? Do you have … uh… is your dad going to wear a kilt, or any uncles, or relatives that are coming? And will— will it be your tartan, or …?

Nikki Our family tartan's not very nice … uh … so no, I don't think we'll probably use the— the— our family tartan – in fact, I know nobody's using our tartan. But … um … we will have quite a few people in kilts. My dad will be in a kilt, and … um … all of the— the— I think basically all of the wedding party will be, so all the ushers will be. And none of them are Scottish, they're all— there's one that's English, one that's … uh … Lithuanian, one that's … um … American … um … and then— Yeah, so they're from everywhere and they're all keen to wear kilts as well. I think they all see it— and we've actually had quite a few guests ask us if they can wear kilts too, just 'cos I think they see it as a bit of fun, something they'll never ev— have another opportunity to do.

Lorna I think— I think it's great when you have an international group of people and you can really open up a country's traditions to— to them. I think it's great when people can get involved in things like that. [*Yeah.*] So it sounds like it'll be fantastic.

Nikki Yeah. I hope so.

Unit 18   Rising to a challenge

Track 50

I went to the Seychelles in October of last year … um … for, sort of, last hurrah before having children and … um … we had a total blast. We re— both really like animals and so we decided to go on this sort of nature jungle walk thing where you start at one end and meet the tortoises and then walk through and see all the different flora and fauna and then end up on the beach and have a barbecue at the end. It was gonna be lovely.

Um, it was very laid back 'cos the Creole culture is not quite as … um … you know, organized as— as we would have liked. So it was sort of like 'this is the trail, this is where you go, and we'll see you at the end.' There was no instruction whatsoever. Um, nothing like 'watch out for these animals', no warning at all. Um, so we sort of did a— we did— we did the jungle walk, guided ourselves through the jungle … um … and the very first thing I noticed, after the tortoises, which I loved, were these spiders the size of my head that were, you know, within three or four feet of our head … um … as we walked. Everywhere, just everywhere – the entire canopy of the jungle was filled with these spiders. They were enormous. We had no idea what kind of spiders they were, if they were gonna jump on us, if they could kill us – we had no idea.

So we just sort of had to proceed … um … and get to the end and trust that they weren't going to kill us. Um, there were a couple of very close calls. My husband is very tall so he had to duck constantly … um … out of fear. They didn't really move or make any motions to jump so we thought we were safe and … um … of course, by the end … um … we sort of said to our guides 'those spiders … uh … by any chance were we taking our lives into our own hands?' And they said, 'Oh no, no, no, totally harmless. You know, they're Palm Spiders, they eat bugs,' these kind of things. Sort of like, we kind of wish we knew that from the beginning, would have been much more enjoyable.

Um, so that was one fun thing. Um, and the other was … uh … we made a habit … uh … on our trip of going into the local village for dinners rather than eating at our hotel 'cos we wanted to experience some different foods and it involved walking along this beautiful white beach … um … that was totally, you know … um … barren of people, it was lovely … um … having dinner and then trying to get back before the sun would set, because there's absolutely no lighting, you know, it's just a beach, there's no … um … lamps or anything. So … um … it was gonna either be pitch black or the sun was gonna guide us home.

One night we stayed out a little bit too late – 'cos the sun set at seven so you're really rushing. Um, and the sun was setting as we were walking along the beach and about half way down the beach it was— it was gone. So it was pitch black on the beach … um … and we were just sort of guided by starlight and moonlight … um … and what we also didn't know was that as soon as the sun set, these crabs emerge and take over the beach. The— Crabs that are the size of— I think they're actually called coconut crabs because they can open coconuts with their huge claws. Um, so that's how big and— and frightening they were. And they t— literally covered every inch of the beach and we had to walk through a sea of them … um … to get home. Um, and hear their, sort of, s— their panicked scrambling and my screams and all this interposed on each other. Um, and they live in the jungle, not in the sea, so they would scurry back into the jungle and crawl over all these dried leaves and make this horrific noise. Um, so there was about five minutes to ten minutes of complete terror on my part – lots of screaming. Um, my husband thought it was hilarious. We got home safely … um … but, you know, learned our lesson to get home on time the next day.

Track 51

Well, I worked at a music festival called Glastonbury. Um, and the work that I did was for a charity and … um … we created a … um … a house that was supposed to be flood-resistant or flood-proof … um … to help festival-goers learn about … um … how different communities around the world were having to adapt to rising sea levels. Um, and we were in a bigger field of a bigger charity.

Um, and so I'd never been to Glastonbury before so it was my first experience. I was very, very excited. Um, and I was going to be there for a total of about ten days … um … because we had to arrive before all the festival-goers arrived … um … and build this structure … uh … by ourselves, which was quite a challenge as we'd never done anything like that before. Um, and so when we arrived, Glastonbury— like, the fields were all pristine and green and the weather was just about okay … um … and so we managed to build the structure and get all organized and then all the festival-goers started to arrive on Wednesday and the weather got increasingly worse and it started to rain every day for a considerable amount of time. And the fields got muddier and muddier and so it just got ridiculous, trying to move around.

But whilst I was working, you know, I had my shifts, you know, working for the charity, and then I had my time off. And so, having never been to the festival before … um … I took advantage and explored all the different stages and all the different areas and it was absolutely amazing. Like, the atmosphere was fantastic— everyone— even though the weather was awful, everyone was really, really happy and excited about being there. And I had some amazing experiences, completely random things where you're kind of walking down and you bump into a group of people in the dark playing musical instruments in a bandstand, just on their own, and all the rain was tipping down around them.

Um, and then I slept in a tent in the … um … staff area of the larger charity we were with in the field. And … um … I found sleeping quite difficult actually, because … um … the noise around you never really stops, so … um … because music kind of continues after the big stages have finished, after the big bands have finished, and the dance tents kinda continue. And then at about ten o'clock in the morning the stages start up again. So … uh … it was quite hard to get any proper rest. Um, but somehow, you know, we managed to keep trucking, keep going, and … um … work our shifts and explore the festival at the same time. And … uh … trudge through the mud and … uh … survive.

Um, and then by the end … um … it was really— it was really sad because on the last day of the festival … um … you know, they have the big, headlining act and … um … you know, massive crowds all congregate on the main stage— around the main stage. And— … um … and then the next day everyone starts to leave. But we weren't leaving because we had to then dismantle … um … the structure that we'd built and collect every single screw we'd used … um … everything, which was all covered in mud. Um, so it was really arduous and hard work to dismantle this structure. And everyone was tired and a bit depressed about the festival being over. You know, several of our team had already left and so it obviously felt like something was ending and all the euphoria and excitement had obviously disappeared by that point. Um, we were all tired and muddy and fed up with the mud.

Um, and that was quite some time ago now and I haven't been back to Glastonbury since. That's not because I was scarred by the mud … um … but … um … I don't know, I guess it's just the window of opportunity hasn't, kind of, opened itself. And I think I would like to go again … um … but I'm a bit of a stickler for home comforts and probably want to … um … go glam camping rather than, like, basic camping. Um, with nice toilets. Um, yeah— so, yeah, I'd like to do it again, yeah, but maybe not work there again.

Unit 19   Holiday destinations

Track 52

Laura   Hey, how was your holiday?

Jude   it was amazing! We had such a ball. Uh, we went to Sydney and then drove down to Melbourne. Have you— have you ever been?

Laura   Yeah, I've been to both. Um, I've been to Sydney on work and I've been there on holiday as well. [*Oh, cool.*] Which part of Sydney did you stay in?

Jude   Well we stayed in the university in— in Glebe, which was really cool to— to see— to see that area 'cos it was quite, sort of, cutting edge. But we spent quite a lot of time down in the centre. We were there for a wedding, actually – my boyfriend's friend was getting married. Um, so they had the reception with a lovely view of the Harbour Bridge. Um, it was around Christmas time so we were there for New Year … um … and spent—

Laura   Must have been hot.

Jude   It was boiling! So we— we were told by someone that … um … we had to go and get a good view of the fireworks sort of from midday, and so we were si— sitting there for twelve hours in the sunshine waiting for all the fireworks to go off. I mean, when they eventually came, it— it was well worth the wait, but my goodness, I had a very burnt nose by the end of the afternoon, I have to … [*Oh, amazing.*] Where— where did you stay when you went?

Laura   Um, my sister was living there for about six months and she had an apartment in Bondi, [*Wow.*] on the far side of Bondi beach [*Mhmm.*] which sounds amazing but it was— the first time I went there was in winter and it's really cold on Bondi in winter, in August for them. So it was kind of windy and really cold [*Oh.*] so it wasn't as glamorous as it sounds.

Jude   We went there actually too and we saw— … um … the minute we arrived they had a shark alert so everyone had to get out of the sea and stand on the sta— sand. Um, but then after that we went for a walk along the— the coastal route to Coogee. Did you do that?

Laura   Oh yeah, that's a really nice beach at Coogee.

Jude   Yeah. That was really special.

Laura   It's a bit easier to swim there, isn't it? [*Mmm, yeah.*] 'cos in Bondi the— the … um … the waves are really high because of the cove.

Jude   Yeah, that's true, 'cos of the— the surfers and so on. But no, you're right, they're— the coves are a lot smaller and … uh … yeah, it's— it's gorgeous. What did you make of Melbourne when you went?

Laura   It's— it's an amazing city, it— well, a town. It … um … it rains a lot – the whole time we were there it rained, so it was quite like a European city. It's very cosmopolitan, nice cafés, nice shops, and some nice beaches as well. It doesn't really have the beach feel like Sydney does [*Mmm, that's true.*] so I think— I've been to Sydney more than I've been to Melbourne, so I think you either like one or the other.

Jude   Yeah, I guess … um … the main beach in Melbourne is Saint— Saint Kilda. Did you go at all to Phi— Phillip Island [*No.*] … um … from Melbourne at all? We went there and … um … went to the— the koala bear sanctuary … um … and also to see the penguins coming in [*Aww.*] … um … at— at sunset [*That's nice.*] which was really quite special.

Laura   Koalas are gorgeous, [*I know.*] I absolutely love koalas. They look like wise little old men!

Jude   Oh no, they— they do. They— they— they've got funny little faces and they— they on— they're only awake for three hours a day, I think, and the rest of the time they're just sleeping or— or eating [*Just looking.*] eucalyptus.

Laura   They do smell like eucalyptus all the time. If— if you get close to them you can just smell eucalyptus.

Jude   Mmm. No, it's true. Did you see any koala bears— sorry, any kangaroos whilst you were there?

Laura   Uh, yeah, we went to … um … we went to a wildlife park in— in Sydney … um … just outside the centre, so they were tame ones and we got to feed them. It's not the same as seeing them in the wild. I've seen them in the wild in Perth— outside Perth [*Oh, wow.*] on the west coast, but I hadn't seen any in the wild on the east coast. I guess it's a bit more populated there.

Jude   Yeah. Did you— did you see any with joeys in their little pouches?

Laura   Yeah, outside Perth, I did. I was outside a visitor centre – oh, it was amazing – there was nobody around 'cos it's in the middle of nowhere … um … along this stretch of coast there was a visitor centre. I was hiding in the shade 'cos it was about 41 degrees at the time and I put on— I was putting on sun lotion in the shade [*Mhmm.*] and I noticed a little kangaroo jump behind the visitor centre in— to— for shade as well. And I looked round— I crept round really quietly and there was about twenty kangaroos hiding in the shade [*Awww.*] and one of them that was closest to me had a little joey in its pouch [*Awww, how cute!*] and as it was looking at me the joey just stuck its head out the pouch. It was so cute.

Jude   Oh, adorable. And talking of the coastal routes, did you do the Great Ocean Road, whilst you were—

Laura   Oh, yeah, that's amazing. [*Oh, it's special, isn't it? It's amazing.*] That's really amazing.

Jude   The route is so windy but it's, you know, it's well worth kind of navigating through to get to see the Twelve Apostles. Did you— did you … um … see them at sunset?

Laura   Oh no, I didn't, I saw them during the day. That must have looked so beautiful at sunset.

Jude   Oh no, it was. It was gorgeous.

Track 53

Megan   So I'm thinking about going to Japan in August. [*Uhuh.*] Um, I was wondering, is that a good time, sort of, weather-wise and …?

Saya   Well, weather-wise, you might know or not but in— on August is kind of— My opinion is it's not a good— good season because there's so much … um … you know, high heat and then it's very, very hot summer in Japan and very humidity, so it's quite … um … different from the … um … summer in Europe. So, because Europe is quite dry and then even if you go to, like, under the shade you can be kind of, you know, much cooler, but in Japan in the summers, everywhere is so, so hot with humid it's gonna be—

Megan That sounds nice!

Saya Oh yeah, but then it— it will be really annoying later on. You very sweating and very sticky, your skins. I not really keen on— I not really recommend you to go.

Megan Oh, okay. Is there— is there anything good on in— in August, or …?

Saya Um, August we have one festival … um … then. It's called Obon. And … um … and that is very … um … traditional or … um … especially if you are go to rural area, they are kind of celebrating, like, really … um … huge. And— But same time … um … all the Obon season we have three days, the all three days most of the shops were in close. [*Oh.*] So— well— some point, if you want really … um … enjoy the festival it will be good time to go but at same time, you kind of want to enjoy more shopping-wise, it's not the, you know, best season to go.

Megan So does everything shut down, or …?

Saya Well, most likely. Like … um … I'm from a really rural area so most of the shop and supermarket will be closed— or actually, it's one or two days. Then if you go to, like, Tokyo, probably it's not closed all the shops, so you can even buy anything to eat. And b— restaurants could be closed but— yeah …

Megan Oh, okay. So does it— so it's celebrated more in rural areas, then. But does it happen everywhere, or …?

Saya Uh, well it's meant to be happen everywhere, but in— you know, people who … uh … live in— in Tokyo, or some like a big place, they're kind of, you know, just working and they don't really follow the kind of traditional festivals. But if you go to rural area, you know, people more … um … thinking, 'Oh, we have to do this f— … um … festival and we have to celebrate this … um … properly'. So, like, my parents … um … especially … um … they never live out of side of their hometown, so on the August they kind of, you know, prepare, 'Oh, Obon is coming a week's time' and then they kind of, you know, preparing everything, so … [*Oh, okay.*] But someone who from Tokyo— or someone who live in Tokyo, they kind of less care, [*Oh, okay.*] yeah, compared to—

Megan So— so round you, people take days off work and— and really build up to it?

Saya Um, they try to be but in— as you may know, Japan is very, you know, busy worker every day. [*Yeah.*] It's quite hard to take a day off, but in— yeah, Obon time, could be … um … more— like … uh … reasonable to get— take—get … um … days off and annual leave. Yeah.

Megan So how do they prepare for it, then? How do your parents prepare?

Saya Uh, well basically— and so … um … thirteenth of August, that is the first day of the festival, so we normally go to the … um … shrine—shr— shrine. And then— and then we just kind of pray and then kind of welcome to my … um … ancestor. Then we literally— well, they already—… um … pa—… uh … passed away but usually we go to the shrine then … um … we kind of receive their— like a soul, ish, and then we bring to our house and they welcome to ancestor and then kind of celebrate. And then fourteenth, we have … um … a kind of … um … traditional dancing in the … uh … garden, [*Oh.*] so, if you have, like, much space. And then we bring some—… um … and cousins, all the relatives and then we having like a traditional meal and then just, you know, [*Oh, wow.*] normal celebration. And then the last day is f— gonna be fifteenth of August so we are going to shrine again and kind of reascending their kind of soul to the shrine— is— do you understand? [*Yeah.*] Yeah. [*Yeah.*] Something like that. [*Okay.*] So it more like a religious thing to me, so yeah …

Megan So is to sort of … um … celebrate your ancestors [*Yeah.*] or pay respects to them [*Exactly.*] or look after them? [*Yeah, yeah.*] All of them? [*Yeah.*] Yeah. Wow. So is that something that tourists, if they're there, can join in with or …?

Saya Yeah. [*Yeah?*] Especially on the Obon season, when I say … um … we are doing like a traditional dance with … um … *yukata* which is kind of— it's not a kimono, but quite similar looks. Uh, so this a very traditional outfit— Japanese outfit [*Yeah.*] so looks like kimono but much, like, lighter because we are wearing in the summer— [*Yeah.*] -the sticky summer. So it's much lighter and the— more…um…casual way, but very traditional so. And because, especially once you are wearing a nice…uh…*yukata* so you can really enjoy it to wear— then you can, you know— even you don't know how to dance but…um…yeah, it's very easy anyway!

Unit 20   Life-changing events

Track 54

The sailing race I took part in was called the ARC, which stands for the Atlantic Race for Cruisers, and is open to anyone who wants to race from the Canaries— the last island in the Canaries all the way through the Atlantic to the island of St Lucia in the Caribbeans. And I took part on a thirty-five-foot yacht and it was a twenty-day voyage.

We had quite heavy winds to start with and for seventy or eighty percent of the voyage in total. The winds are measured on a Beaufort scale which is force one up to force twelve, force twelve being more or less a hurricane, force one looking at the sea and it's like a mirror almost. And we had force six to force seven all the way through, so quite rough. But the— you're on the trade winds which means you— that you had the wind behind you and in the old days the— the— the tea clippers etcetera, such large sailing ships, would use those winds to trade effectively around the world.

And the best bits were— honestly, the isolation was just fantastic. Because once you've left the— the start line you head on into the night and you can see the— the port lights and the starboard lights from the other ships but very slowly over the course of the hours, they become more and more faint and you realize you are out there by yourself, and there's no one that's gonna come— be able to come and pick you up or— or help you if you do run into trouble. Uh, or at least no one that can get to you very quickly. So your comfort zone is—…uh…you're out of your comfort zone. You'll find that the only way of reaching anyone back home is satellite telephone so if there was— if, for example…uh…you— there was a— there was a death on the ship, the satellite telephone would have been used. Um, but generally— you— you could— we could…um…log into…uh…Internet facilities via that satellite phone but, you know, it was expensive, it was probably about six pounds a minute, so you— you would limit your usage of that technology.

Uh, there were lo— lots of other bits of technology that were fantastic, of course, along the way. But your— the— the GPS is— is just not as…uh…functional as it— you'd find it would be if you were nearer land because the amount of satellites that are in the sky…uh…most of which are owned— owned by America – I think one satellite's owned by China – and you have the— the— that— that technology which we get used to on the road, we get used to around the coast, just— just isn't there. So you have to start to…um…rely on other ways of— of— other means of navigation. And fortunately we were taught how to use the sextant…uh…on board, which is a t— time-old way of…uh…measuring the sun when it is at its zenith and…uh…then, looking at the horizon, you can start to work out where you are in terms of latitude and longitude. Having said that, you know, you still can get these files downloaded…um…by using the Internet for a few minutes just to get a rough idea of your position…uh…in— in— in— in the…uh…greater scheme of things. And obviously you're plotting it on a chart all the way along.

I hadn't done it before and so I was very excited by it. I had raced a lot down off the south coast with the skipper, and he obviously thought that I'd be okay as crew. Um, I have done little voyages around. I say little, you know, they're— to— to the—…uh… uninitiated they might sound a bit larger, but I have crossed Biscay twice on— on yachts, and I have crossed … uh … the channel a few times on yachts, and I got to know the ropes, quite literally…uh…around Chichester harbour…uh…initially when I started sailing. So I was— I was au fait with what was going on.

I would definitely do it again. I would recommend it to anyone. It's a fantastic experience, particularly because you are in— tho— those—…um…those— those latitudes where the weather starts to pick up and— and you actually get some sunshine which is— the sinking— sinking sun into the sea every night is just one of those wonderful visions that stays with you forever.

Track 55

Then, as the months had gone on, you know, all this time— all this time I'm on the transplant list, so at any time I could have— you know, I was waiting for a phone call but—...um...to say, you know, there was—a— a new kidney, but you— I just sort of got on with it and in a way forgot about it, you know, thinking 'oh, I'm just gonna get on, it'll happen'. And I think just being that bit younger I didn't really have the worries of anything, just thinking 'oh, it'll come eventually'. Both my parents were tested to— to— to give...um...you know, to give their kidney, but they're not the same blood group as me. In fact, nor's my brother. And I suppose I am naturally born to them, apparently, although I'm the only one with a different blood group – I really don't know! And my brother is younger than me so...um...there was no chance of, you know, whipping his kidney out. But my parents, they weren't a match, so I had to wait for somebody else – you know, see what— what was gonna happen.

Just at the time when I did find out about a kidney, I was advised that I was gonna have to start doing dialysis four times a day instead of three. But anyway, luckily for me, just before this happened I got a phone call, one Sunday morning. I was just about— I was— I remember 'cos I was eating a bowl of Cheerios and I was— my friend had come to— we were gonna go out riding, and she used to keep her horse just down the way from me and...um...we'd just— she'd just come to call and I was eating my— my Cheerios ready to have my breakfast – ...uh...well, having my breakfast, ready to go out riding. And I got the phone call. And I remember 'cos the phone's on the wall and then my mother, she answered the phone and just went, 'It's for you'.

So this doctor, and I can't remember for the life of me what he's called, but he was Scottish, he was very nice, he went, 'Rachael, we have a kidney just for you, you need to be in in twenty minutes.' So I was— I was shaking a— and I thought, 'Well, I need to finish my Cheerios' because I knew I wouldn't be able to eat for ages and I— I did— I had— you know, I like my food. So I thought, 'finish your Cheerios 'cos you're not gonna be able to eat for ages'. So I was sh— I remember my hand was shaking, I'm eating these Cheerios. Caroline, my friend, was there and everyone was in a spin and—...um...and— and then I— mother took me over to the hospital and when I went to the hospital I was the only one there, I was the only one called for this kidney. This kidney apparently was the perfect match for me. And...um...and it did actually— it has proved to be.

So, I went...um...in for the kidney on July 16th and I went to have— in for the transplant on July 17th, the next day. Um, and I— when I went for the transplant, I came round...um...and it took about ten days for the transplant to kick off – it just wasn't starting. My body wasn't, I don't think, particularly rejecting it, but it wasn't starting and it wasn't going. So I had to go on the dialysis machine to see it and— to see— to— they could kick-start the kidney to go. And I had, I think it was probably steroid injections, something like that, some injections to— to— to really jumpstart this kidney to get it going 'cos it wasn't going at first. But— and it— that was a real worry and that was quite stressful 'cos I thought, you know, you've waited— you know, I'd waited, you know, like, nearly seven months...um...and this kidney's just got to kicks— just got to go, and I'm, like, 'please, please make this kidney kick-start. And then, it just did. It just kick-started, it never looked back. And then as it kick-started on and it started to function properly, I was just starting to feel well, more well, well, well and just sort of really, you know, full of life and full of energy that I hadn't really been before. Um, and just feel so much better.

Track 56

I think, you know, it's— I mean, I can understand. It's very, very stressful when you're— you've lost a loved one, you're in the hospital and they're, you know, they w— saying, 'well, would you like to donate any of their organs?' Well you— I can imagine your first thought would be 'no, no, leave them in— no, no, no,' you know? But now I think they've got, sort of, the— bit more training's gone into it so coordinators— transplant coordi— coordinators can talk to families and really und— help them understand, you know. 'Cos— And even sometimes when it's been the patient's wishes, the family have said no. But I can completely understand where families are coming from when they've lost someone. It must be so hard. And then from my side of the fence, and if— if anyone has a child who needs an organ, it's like— you don't, you know, you don't need it when you go and there's so many— you know, you can give a life and you could help somebody live a full life, you— you know, but it's— it's a difficult time when you've been bereaved, I think. But...um...you— I think you'll always be grateful for that person, even though you don't know who she— who she is, but I suppose she's there.

Collins Also available

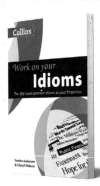